BENJAMIN HARMON

DISGUISED IN DAYLIGHT

The True Story of Ellen and William Craft's 1,000-Mile Escape from Slavery—and the Love That Defied a Nation

Copyright © 2025 by Benjamin Harmon

All rights reserved. No part of this publication may be reproduced, stored or transmitted in any form or by any means, electronic, mechanical, photocopying, recording, scanning, or otherwise without written permission from the publisher. It is illegal to copy this book, post it to a website, or distribute it by any other means without permission.

Benjamin Harmon asserts the moral right to be identified as the author of this work.

Benjamin Harmon has no responsibility for the persistence or accuracy of URLs for external or third-party Internet Websites referred to in this publication and does not guarantee that any content on such Websites is, or will remain, accurate or appropriate.

Designations used by companies to distinguish their products are often claimed as trademarks. All brand names and product names used in this book and on its cover are trade names, service marks, trademarks and registered trademarks of their respective owners. The publishers and the book are not associated with any product or vendor mentioned in this book. None of the companies referenced within the book have endorsed the book.

First edition

This book was professionally typeset on Reedsy.
Find out more at reedsy.com

We did not run away; we walked away in broad daylight, with the sun for witness and love for our passport."

— Ellen Craft, letter to the
Anti-Slavery Bugle, 1851

Contents

Prologue — 1

I Part One

1. Born in Bondage — 7
2. The Cabinet Maker's Apprentice — 15
3. CHAPTER 3 A Marriage in Secret — 24

II Part Two

4. Mr. William Johnson & Valet — 33
5. Savannah: The Captain's Doubt — 43
6. Charleston: The Dinner Table Trap — 54
7. The Overnight Train to Freedom — 63
8. Philadelphia: First Breath of Freedom — 71

III Part Three

9. Boston: The Abolitionist Stage — 83
10. The Fugitive Slave Act — 90
11. Boston: The Siege — 96
12. Atlantic Crossing: Third Escape — 101

IV Part Four

13. London: Reinventing Freedom — 109

14	The American War from Afar	116
15	Return to Georgia: The Dream	121
16	The Burning of Woodville	126
17	Last Harvest	130
18	EPILOGUE Tracks in the Snow	134
19	APPENDICES	138

Prologue

The Plan in the Dark

Macon, Georgia – Christmas Eve 1848

The candle guttered in its tin holder, a single tongue of flame trembling against the night. Outside, the plantation bells had long since stilled; inside the cabinet shop, the air hung thick with the scent of pine shavings and turpentine. Ellen Craft knelt on the packed-earth floor, her knees pressing into the sawdust that still carried the day's warmth. In her right hand she held a pair of tailor's shears—borrowed, never returned—its blades catching the candlelight like a sliver of moon.

She drew a breath that tasted of resin and fear, then brought the shears to the nape of her neck. The first lock fell away with a soft *snip*, curling like a dark ribbon across her wrist. Another followed, then another, until the floor was strewn with the evidence of her transformation. Each severed strand was a renunciation: of the house girl who poured tea for the mistress, of the child who had once been told her lightness was a curse, of the woman who had learned to read faces better than books because books were forbidden. The hair that remained—cropped close, uneven, boyish—would be hidden beneath a beaver hat tomorrow. Tonight, it was the first cut toward freedom.

Across the narrow room, William Craft crouched over a splintered crate, his broad shoulders hunched against the chill that seeped through the plank walls. A scrap of brown paper—torn from the bottom of a grocery list—lay beneath his charcoal stub. With the precision of the cabinetmaker he had become, he traced the rail lines he had memorized from overheard conversations: Macon to Savannah, 190 miles; Savannah to Charleston by steamer; Charleston northward, if God and the conductors allowed. His fingers, calloused from planes and chisels, moved with the sureness of a man drafting a cathedral. Every mile was a joint to be fitted, every river crossing a dovetail that must not fail.

He paused, glancing up. Ellen's reflection wavered in the cracked mirror propped against a stack of walnut boards. The candlelight painted her cheekbones gold, her eyes obsidian. For a moment, the shop's clutter—the half-finished wardrobe, the scent of linseed oil, the distant hoot of a train whistle—faded. There was only her.

"Ellen," he said, voice low, "you certain?"

She set the shears aside and rose, the hem of her calico dress brushing the shorn curls. "I was certain the first time you looked at me like I was already free."

He crossed the room in three strides, the floorboards creaking beneath his bare feet. When he reached her, he did not embrace her—not yet. Instead, he lifted a fallen lock of hair, rolling it between thumb and forefinger as if testing the grain of mahogany. Then, gently, he tucked it into the breast pocket of his osnaburg shirt, directly over his heart.

"Evidence," he murmured. "For the children we'll have one day. Proof their mother was brave enough to cut her own chains."

The candle sputtered, throwing their shadows tall against the wall. Outside, a dog barked once, then thought better of it. Ellen reached for the bundle she had sewn in secret: a gentleman's coat of bottle-green broadcloth, a sling of white linen, a pair of spectacles with tinted lenses. She laid them across the crate like a surgeon arranging instruments.

William unrolled the paper fully. At the bottom, beneath the charcoal routes, he had drawn a tiny heart pierced by an arrow. Beneath it, in letters so small they could only be read by someone who already knew they were there: *E & W – 1,000 miles or bust.*

Ellen leaned over his shoulder, her breath warm against his ear. "Tomorrow," she said, "I will be Mr. William Johnson, Esquire, of parts unknown. Invalid. Deaf in the right ear. You will be my body servant. And if anyone asks why a gentleman travels with only one slave—"

"—I'll tell them the rest are too sickly for the journey," he finished. The corner of his mouth lifted, the closest he came to a smile in weeks.

She touched the heart on the map. "And if they ask why the gentleman cannot write his own name?"

"You'll cough into your sling. I'll say the fever took your hand." He covered her fingers with his own. "We've rehearsed it a hundred times."

"Not the part where we live," she whispered.

The candle chose that moment to drown in its own wax. Darkness rushed in, sudden and complete. For a heartbeat, they were only breath and heartbeat in the void. Then William struck a second lucifer against the crate, and the flame leapt back to life, smaller now, more desperate.

Ellen lifted the coat. The sleeves were too long—she had measured by stealing glances at the master's son—but the weight of it felt right. She slipped her arms inside, the broadcloth cool against her skin. William adjusted the collar, his knuckles brushing the pulse at her throat.

"Mirror," she said.

He turned it toward her. The reflection that stared back was a stranger: a slight young man with a bandaged arm, spectacles perched on a nose too delicate for the face they framed. The transformation was not perfect—the jaw too soft, the lips too full—but in the half-light of a train car, with illness as an excuse, it might suffice.

William stepped behind her, resting his chin atop her cropped head. In the mirror, they were master and slave, the roles they had been born to invert.

"Tomorrow," he said, "we board the four o'clock to Savannah. If the clerk asks for papers—"

"—I'll be too feeble to produce them."

"If the captain refuses—"

"—you'll offer double fare for the invalid's comfort."

"If they discover us—"

She turned in his arms, the coat swirling like a cape. "Then we die together. But not tonight."

The train whistle sounded again, farther off, a mournful promise carried on the wind. William extinguished the candle with a pinch. In the sudden dark, their lips found each other—urgent, reverent, the first kiss that belonged to no one but themselves. When they parted, Ellen's voice was steady as winter iron.

"Tomorrow we ride as master and slave," she said. "Or we die together."

Outside, the stars over Macon kept their ancient watch, indifferent to the two souls who had just drawn the blueprint of their liberty on a scrap of stolen paper and sealed it with a kiss.

Part One

CHAINS

One

Born in Bondage

Ellen – *Macon, Georgia, 1826*

The first cry that announced Ellen Craft to the world was muffled by the heavy damask draperies of the master's bedroom. It was late summer, 1826, and the air in the Big House on Mulberry Street hung thick with heat and the metallic scent of blood. Eliza, the enslaved woman whose body had just been rent by childbirth, lay spent upon a corn-shuck mattress shoved into the corner. No doctor attended her; the midwife was another slave, Aunt Dicey, whose hands trembled from exhaustion and whose remedies were limited to sips of sassafras tea and whispered prayers.

Colonel Ira Smith, the child's legal father, stood at the window in his linen waistcoat, watching the dust rise from the wagon road. He had not entered the room since the labor began. When the infant's wail finally pierced the hush, he turned only long enough to confirm what the mirror had already told him: the baby was light—too light. Her skin carried the translucent glow of fresh cream; her hair, damp and curling, was the color of weak coffee. The colonel's mouth tightened. Another "fancy girl," another complication.

Ellen's mother, Eliza, was herself the product of the colonel's earlier indiscretion with a house servant named Maria. Eliza had been raised in the Big House, trained to pour tea with the grace of a Charleston belle and to anticipate the mistress's moods before they surfaced. Her complexion—barely darker than the colonel's own daughters—had been both her currency and her curse. Now, holding the squirming bundle to her breast, Eliza felt the weight of generations settle on the child's tiny shoulders. She named her Ellen, after no one in particular, because the name sounded free.

By the time Ellen could toddle, the Big House had become her universe. She learned to navigate its polished floors in bare feet, to curtsey when the mistress passed, to carry silver trays heavier than herself without spilling a drop of syllabub. The colonel's legitimate daughters—Maria and Frances—were her half-sisters in blood but worlds apart in station. They wore silk slippers; Ellen wore hand-me-down calico. They learned French verbs; Ellen learned to read the weather in the mistress's eyes.

Yet the mirror betrayed her daily. At age five, she stood on a stool in the pantry, peering into a cracked hand-glass while Aunt Dicey braided her hair. "You got the devil's own luck, child," the old woman muttered. "Light enough to pass, dark enough to hang." The words lodged in Ellen's mind like burrs. She began to notice how the overseer's gaze lingered, how the mistress's mouth pursed when Ellen entered a room. She learned to make herself small, to speak only when spoken to, to disappear into doorways.

In the slave quarters behind the Big House, the contrast was stark. There, children her age wore osnaburg shirts and played with whittled sticks. Their skin drank the sun; Ellen's blistered and peeled. When she ventured out at dusk to fetch water, the field hands stared. "That the colonel's yaller gal?" they'd whisper. Ellen would clutch the cedar bucket tighter and hurry back, the word *yaller* echoing like a slap.

By 1835, when Ellen was nine, the Macon Telegraph carried advertisements that might have been written for her future:

FOR SALE: A likely mulatto girl, age 9, house-raised, accustomed to waiting, warranted sound. Apply at the Eagle Tavern. —*Macon Telegraph*, 12 March 1835

The colonel never placed such an ad—Ellen was too valuable in the house—but the threat was implicit. Every birthday was a reprieve, every growth spurt a reminder that time was a ledger. When the mistress took ill in

1837, Ellen was promoted to personal nurse, sleeping on a pallet outside the bedroom door. She learned to administer laudanum with a steady hand, to read the doctor's Latin prescriptions by candlelight, to anticipate death before it announced itself.

In the quiet hours, when the house slept, Ellen would creep to the library. The colonel's books—Scott, Byron, the *North American Review*—stood in solemn rows behind glass. She traced the letters with her finger, mouthing shapes she could not sound. One night, she found a discarded primer beneath the desk. The cover was torn, but the alphabet marched across the page like soldiers. She hid it in her apron pocket and carried it to the attic, where moonlight through a chink in the shingles became her only teacher.

Years later, she would recall the taste of that stolen knowledge—bitter as green persimmons, sweet as stolen honey. It was the first time she understood that the world beyond the Big House was larger than the colonel's whim, that words could be weapons sharper than any overseer's lash.

But in 1826, as Eliza rocked her newborn daughter and the colonel turned back to the window, Ellen's destiny was already inscribed in the ledgers: *Property of Ira Smith, valued at $400.* The ink was barely dry.

William – Macon, Georgia, 1824–1840

The cotton field began where the Big House lawn ended, a brutal demarcation drawn by a split-rail fence and the overseer's whip. On a sweltering July morning in 1824, somewhere between the second and third bell, William Craft drew his first breath beneath a lean-to of pine boughs. His mother, Milly, had been granted no respite from the rows; she squatted in the furrow, one hand braced against a cotton stalk, the other clutching the newborn to her sweat-soaked bosom. The infant's cry was thin, quickly swallowed by the cicadas' drone and the rhythmic *thwack* of hoes.

Milly was field property, valued in the plantation ledger at $350. Her husband—William's father—had been sold south two seasons earlier, a transaction noted in the same crabbed hand that recorded bushels of cotton and barrels of turpentine. The child was simply *"boy, likely, born of Milly."* No surname, no ceremony. The midwife, a root-doctor named Aunt Phebe, cut the cord with a dull blade and tied it with a strip of burlap. "He got lungs," she declared. "He'll need 'em."

William's world was measured in rows. By age four, he toddled behind his mother, dragging a smaller sack, learning to pluck the bolls without pricking his fingers on the sharp burrs. The sun branded his skin the color of river clay; his hair grew tight and springy, a helmet against the heat. Unlike Ellen, whose lightness kept her indoors, William's darkness consigned him to the fields from dawn to dusk. His hands, by seven, were already mapped with calluses.

The Macon Telegraph of the 1830s carried notices that might have been his future:

VALUABLE FIELD HAND: Boy, 12 years, stout, accustomed to cotton, warranted sound and title clear. Sold to settle estate. —*Macon Telegraph,* 9 October 1836

William's master, Dr. Robert Collins, was a physician who owned three plantations and a pharmacy on Cotton Avenue. He kept meticulous records: *"William, age 10, 4'6", 75 lbs, $450 valuation."* The boy's worth increased with every inch of height, every pound of muscle. When fever swept the quarters in 1832, William survived—another entry: *"Boy William, recovered, no loss of labor."*

At twelve, he was promoted to water boy, a position that allowed him to roam the edges of the fields. He learned to read the overseer's moods in the set of his shoulders, to anticipate the lash by the twitch of a wrist. He also learned the geography of escape: the Ocmulgee River's bend, the stage road to Savannah, the whistle of the Western & Atlantic Railroad under construction north of town. These were fragments, stored like tools in a cabinet he had not yet built.

In 1838, Dr. Collins decided to diversify. He apprenticed William to a Macon cabinetmaker, Mr. Ira H. Smith—Ellen's future master, though neither child knew it then. The arrangement was economic: Collins kept ownership, Smith paid a yearly hire of $125, and William learned a trade that might increase his value. The boy was sent to live in the cabinet shop's loft, a narrow space above the sawdust and varnish.

Here, for the first time, William slept beneath a roof that did not leak.

He learned to plane walnut until it gleamed like water, to dovetail joints so tight a blade could not slip between. Mr. Smith, a stern Baptist who forbade swearing, allowed William to handle the finest tools—rosewood chisels, brass-backed saws—because the boy's hands were steady and his eye true. In exchange, William worked from 5 a.m. to 9 p.m., ate cornbread and molasses, and was locked in the loft each night.

The shop became his university. He listened to white apprentices read aloud from *The Georgia Journal*, memorizing headlines about Texas annexation and nullification debates. He learned numbers by measuring lumber: *"Three boards, 12 feet, 2 inches thick—$1.80."* When a customer left a tattered almanac, William hid it beneath his pallet and traced the letters by moonlight. W-I-L-L-I-A-M. The name felt like a key.

By 1840, at sixteen, he stood nearly six feet, broad through the shoulders, his hands scarred but precise. Dr. Collins visited the shop quarterly to inspect his investment. "Boy's worth $1,200 now," he told Smith, running a thumb along a flawless mahogany joint. "Might sell him to a Savannah factor—city wages are higher."

The threat was casual, delivered over a glass of Madeira. William, sanding a tabletop nearby, heard every word. That night, in the loft, he carved his initials into a scrap of pine: *W.C.* Beneath it, he added a tiny rail line—two parallel scratches and a cross-tie. A map, or a prayer.

He did not yet know that, six miles away, a light-skinned girl named Ellen was learning to pour tea without trembling. He did not know that their paths would converge at an auction block in 1846, or that the skills he honed in this shop—precision, patience, the ability to see a finished form inside rough wood—would one day craft their freedom.

But in the loft, with the scent of linseed oil and the distant whistle of a locomotive, William Craft began to dream in straight lines and perfect joints.

Collision – Macon Auction Yard, February 1846

The Macon auction yard on Cherry Street stank of fear and horse dung. It was the third Saturday in February 1846, and the sky hung low and gray, the kind of cold that bit through osnaburg and wool alike. A crowd of white men—planters in broadcloth, factors in beaver hats, speculators with ledgers tucked under their arms—milled beneath the auctioneer's platform. Slaves stood in a ragged line along the fence, wrists roped loosely, eyes fixed on the mud.

Ellen Craft, now twenty, had been marched here from the Big House at dawn. Her mistress, Eliza Collins (née Smith), had married Dr. Robert Collins's son and inherited Ellen as part of the dowry. The marriage had soured; debts mounted; the solution was liquidation. Ellen wore her best calico dress, the one she had starched herself, but her hands were raw from scrubbing floors the night before. She stood between a field hand named Big Tom and a cook called Aunt Sukey, her pulse hammering so loudly she feared the auctioneer could hear it.

William Craft, twenty-two, arrived in a separate wagon. Dr. Collins had decided to sell him outright—city cabinetmakers were fetching $1,500 in Savannah, and the doctor needed cash for a new gin. William's wrists bore the faint scars of iron from a brief, failed escape attempt at fifteen; otherwise, he was prime: tall, muscular, skilled. He wore the same osnaburg shirt he had slept in, the *W.C.* carved into his pallet now a secret memory.

The auctioneer, a florid man named Mr. Nesbit, climbed the platform with a glass of toddy in one hand and a cowhide whip in the other. "Lot One!" he bellowed. "Likely field buck, twenty-five, sound as a dollar!" Big Tom shuffled forward, sold for $900 to a rice planter from Darien. Ellen's stomach lurched. She was Lot Seven.

William was Lot Nine.

Between them, a boy of ten wept openly. The crowd laughed. Ellen closed her eyes and recited the alphabet she had taught herself in the attic—*A, B, C*—a talisman against the moment her name was called.

"Lot Seven!" Nesbit roared. "Fancy house girl, mulatto, age twenty, trained in all domestic arts—sewing, nursing, waiting table. Warranted virtuous and obedient. Who'll start at five hundred?"

Ellen stepped onto the block. The platform creaked beneath her slight weight. She kept her gaze on the horizon, beyond the crowd, where the Ocmulgee River glinted like a blade. Hands shot up: $600, $700, $800. A Savannah hotelier bid $1,000. A Macon lawyer countered $1,100. Then a new voice, calm and deliberate, cut through the din.

"Twelve hundred."

The crowd turned. Dr. John R. Collins—Ellen's current master—stood at the rear, flanked by his wife. The bid was a formality; he was buying his own property to transfer to his daughter as a wedding gift. The gavel fell. Ellen was sold to herself, in a manner of speaking. She stepped down, legs trembling, and was led to the side bench.

William watched from the line. He had seen fancy girls sold before—paraded, prodded, priced like porcelain. But something in Ellen's carriage—the way she held her chin despite the tremor in her hands—snagged his attention. When their eyes met across the yard, it was not recognition but resonance: two souls who had learned to measure freedom in stolen inches.

"Lot Nine!" Nesbit shouted. "Cabinetmaker, age twenty-two, trained by Mr. Ira Smith himself. Can read figures, write a bill, turn a leg on a table finer than Sheraton. Start at eight hundred!"

William mounted the block. He stood straight, shoulders squared, the way Mr. Smith had taught him to present a finished piece. The bidding climbed fast: $1,000, $1,200, $1,300. A Savannah factor in a silk waistcoat raised his cane: "Fourteen hundred!" Dr. Collins countered: "Fifteen!" The factor hesitated, then shook his head.

"Sold to Dr. Collins for fifteen hundred dollars!" Nesbit slammed the gavel. William stepped down, the rope around his wrists suddenly heavier.

As he passed the bench, Ellen looked up. Their gazes locked again—this time longer, deliberate. In that shared second, the auction yard's clamor faded. William saw the intelligence in her eyes, the defiance cloaked in stillness. Ellen saw the steadiness in his, the craftsman's calm that had survived the whip.

Neither spoke. Words were dangerous here. But William inclined his head, the smallest bow a slave could offer without drawing notice. Ellen answered with a flicker of her eyelids—*I see you.*

Dr. Collins collected his purchases. Ellen was sent back to the Big House to pack her mistress's trunks. William was returned to the cabinet shop, now under the younger Collins's ownership. Their paths would not cross again for months, but the seed was planted.

That night, in the loft above the shop, William took out his carving knife and added a second set of initials beneath his own: *E.C.* The letters were tiny, hidden in the grain of a scrap of walnut. He did not know her name yet, only that she had looked at him as if he were already free.

In the Big House attic, Ellen unfolded the primer she had kept since childhood. She turned to a blank page and, with a stolen stub of pencil, wrote a single word: *WILLIAM.* She stared at it until the candle burned low, then hid the book beneath a loose floorboard.

The Macon Telegraph the following week carried the notice:

SOLD: At public auction, 17 February 1846—one fancy house girl, Ellen, $1,200; one cabinetmaker, William, $1,500. Both warranted sound. J. Nesbit, Auctioneer.

The ink was dry, the transaction complete. But in the quiet spaces between ledger lines, two lives had begun to converge.

Two

The Cabinet Maker's Apprentice

Macon, 1846–1847 – *The Shop and the Ledger*
The cabinet shop on Poplar Street stood two stories tall, its brick facade blackened by the smoke of passing locomotives. Inside, the air was a perpetual haze of walnut dust and beeswax, the rhythmic *scrape* of planes and the *thunk* of mallets providing a cadence more reliable than any clock. William Craft, newly purchased for $1,500, crossed the threshold on March 1, 1846, his few possessions—a spare shirt, a whittled flute, the walnut scrap with *W.C.* and *E.C.*—tied in a bandanna.

Mr. Ira H. Smith, the proprietor, was a spare man with a ledger for a heart. He inspected William the way he inspected lumber: for knots, for warps, for potential. "You'll sleep in the loft," he said, pointing to a ladder. "Work starts at five. Supper's cornbread and what you catch. No liquor, no women, no wandering after curfew. Break a tool, you pay for it out of hire." The hire—$150 per year, paid to Dr. Collins—was noted in the same column as glue and varnish.

William nodded. He had expected worse.

The shop employed three white apprentices—Jedediah, Caleb, and young Tommy Pike, age fourteen, freckled and sharp-tongued. They eyed William with the casual contempt reserved for property that could outwork them. But within a week, William's hands proved their worth. He could joint a drawer so seamlessly that the seam vanished; he could turn a table leg with the symmetry of a compass rose. Mr. Smith watched, then grunted approval—the highest praise he gave.

By April, William had earned a privilege: Sunday afternoons off, provided the week's orders were filled. He used the time to walk the rail yard, memorizing schedules posted on the depot wall. The Western & Atlantic ran north to Atlanta; the Macon & Western south to Savannah. He traced the routes with his finger, committing distances to memory: *Macon to Savannah, 190 miles; 10 hours by rail and steamer.* Numbers were safer than words.

In the loft, he kept a secret ledger of his own. On scraps of sandpaper, he recorded earnings: *April 15 – repaired highboy for Mrs. Lamar, $3 credit.* The credits were imaginary—Mr. Smith pocketed the cash—but the act of writing gave William ownership of his labor. He hid the scraps beneath a loose floorboard, alongside the walnut initial piece.

Tommy Pike, the youngest apprentice, became an unlikely ally. The boy was quick with figures but slow with tools; William, precise with tools but forbidden books, struck a bargain. After supper, when Mr. Smith retired to his parlor Bible, Tommy would climb the ladder with a primer or a tattered *Macon Messenger.* In exchange for help planing a troublesome cherry board, he taught William to sound out syllables by lantern light.

"Cat," Tommy whispered, pointing to the page. "C-a-t," William repeated, his tongue thick with the effort. "Good. Now 'hat.'" "H-a-t." "Put 'em together." "Cat… hat." William's grin split the gloom. The words were clumsy, but they were his.

By midsummer 1846, William could read simple bills of sale and write his name in a firm, slanted hand. Tommy brought harder texts: a discarded almanac, a tract on the Mexican War. William devoured them, tracing maps of Texas and California—places where a man might disappear. He practiced signatures: *William Craft, Cabinetmaker.* The flourish felt like contraband.

Down the street, in the Big House attic, Ellen Craft was engaged in parallel subversion. Her mistress, now Mrs. John R. Collins, had taken to Savannah for the season, leaving Ellen in charge of the household sewing. Bolts of broadcloth, linen, and silk filled the storeroom; needles, thread, and patterns were her currency. At night, when the house slept, Ellen climbed the narrow stairs to the attic gable. Moonlight through the vent provided her only lamp.

She had measured the master's son, young Master James, while he slept off a fever: shoulder to wrist, 26 inches; collar to hem, 32 inches. From these stolen dimensions, she cut a gentleman's coat—bottle-green broadcloth, lined with silk scavenged from an old ball gown. The sleeves were deliberately long; the collar high. She stitched a sling from white linen, wide enough to conceal a hand that must not write. Green-tinted spectacles, purchased from a peddler with coins saved from mending the mistress's lace, completed the kit.

Ellen worked with the precision of a conspirator. Each seam was a promise: *This will carry us north.* She practiced signatures in the dust of the attic floor—*Mr. William Johnson*—erasing them with her bare foot before dawn. The name was arbitrary, chosen because it sounded prosperous and vague. She rehearsed ailments: a rheumatic arm, partial deafness, a cough that excused conversation.

The disguises were hidden in a cedar chest beneath bolts of unused muslin. No one entered the attic; the mistress feared spiders. Ellen's only witness was the primer she had kept since childhood, now swollen with new pages: train schedules copied from the *Macon Telegraph*, distances calculated in stolen moments.

William and Ellen were still strangers, separated by six blocks and the chasm of bondage. But in the quiet hours, their preparations converged. William learned to read the world's grammar; Ellen learned to rewrite her body's. The cabinet shop and the attic became laboratories of liberty, each stitch and syllable a step toward the same impossible door.

Macon, 1847–1848 – Privileges, Signals, and the First Thread

The year 1847 arrived on the wheels of the Macon & Western Railroad, its iron shriek now a daily anthem over Poplar Street. The line had extended to Savannah by spring, and with it came a flood of orders: mahogany sideboards for coastal planters, rosewood secretaries for factors' wives, cherry highboys to grace steamboat salons. Mr. Smith's shop hummed from dawn past dusk;

DISGUISED IN DAYLIGHT

William Craft, at twenty-three, had become the linchpin.

His skill had earned him a second privilege: the key to the tool crib. Mr. Smith, trusting the slave's honesty more than his white apprentices', handed over the brass key on a leather thong. "Mind the augers," he warned. "Lose one, and it's fifty lashes." William accepted the key with a nod, but that night he used it to file a duplicate from a scrap of iron. The original hung at his neck; the copy, wrapped in oilcloth, joined the walnut initials beneath the loft floorboard. A key was a promise.

Tommy Pike, now fifteen and gangly, had grown bold. He smuggled in *The Liberator*—abolitionist sheets mailed from Boston to a sympathetic merchant. Hidden inside a hollowed-out plank, the newspapers reached William on Sunday evenings. He read by the loft's single window, tracing William Lloyd Garrison's fiery editorials with a finger that still smelled of linseed oil. *"I will be heard!"* Garrison thundered. William mouthed the words, tasting their weight. He began to write in the margins: *One day.*

Across town, Ellen's world had narrowed to the attic and the sewing room. The mistress had returned from Savannah pregnant and peevish; Ellen's days were consumed with laying in infant linens. But the nights were hers. She had progressed from copying train schedules to sketching maps on brown paper—routes north via Charleston, Wilmington, Richmond. She calculated fares: *Cabin passage to Charleston, $6; steerage, $3.50.* She practiced her gentleman's signature until the loops were confident, the slant authoritative.

In July 1847, the paths of William and Ellen brushed for the first time since the auction. The occasion was the Fourth of July parade—slave holiday, white spectacle. Dr. Collins allowed his house servants to watch from the Big House porch; Mr. Smith granted William leave to deliver a repaired desk to the courthouse square. As the brass band marched past, William carried the desk on his shoulder, sweat cutting channels through the sawdust on his neck. Ellen stood at the porch rail, a tray of lemonade balanced on her hip.

Their eyes met across the crowd. No nod, no smile—too dangerous. But William shifted the desk so the brass plate faced her: *Craft & Co., Cabinetmakers.* Ellen's gaze flicked to the lettering, then back to his face. She lifted the tray slightly, tilting it so the sunlight caught the silver pitcher.

A signal: *I see you.* William's heart hammered louder than the drums. He passed on, but the image of her—calico dress, steady hands, eyes that held a question—burned into memory.

That night, in the loft, he carved a tiny silver pitcher into the walnut scrap, beside the initials. In the attic, Ellen stitched a strip of green broadcloth into a narrow band—wide enough to tie around a wrist, subtle enough to pass as a sweat rag. She pressed it between the pages of her primer, next to the map labeled *Route North*.

By winter 1847, William's literacy had advanced to ciphering. Tommy taught him fractions using lumber measurements: *"Three boards, 7/8 inch thick, 12 feet long—how many feet?"* William solved it in his head, then wrote the answer in sawdust. Mr. Smith, discovering the calculation, promoted him to foreman over the apprentices—a perilous elevation. Jedediah and Caleb muttered, but the work spoke louder. William now signed delivery tickets: *Received in good order, W. Craft.*

Ellen's breakthrough came in January 1848. The mistress, confined by a difficult pregnancy, demanded a new dressing gown. Ellen was sent to the mercantile for silk. There, behind the counter, stood Tommy Pike's older sister, Ruth, a clerk with abolitionist sympathies. Ruth slipped Ellen a folded paper with the silk: a page torn from a children's speller. *"For your nephew,"* she whispered. Ellen tucked it into her bosom.

That night, in the attic, she sounded out the words by candlelight: *"The cat sat on the mat."* Simple, childish, revolutionary. She wrote them in the margin of her map, then added her own sentence: *"The Crafts will sit free."* The possessive—*the Crafts*—was premature, but it felt inevitable.

Spring 1848 brought a third privilege for William: permission to attend the Methodist church's colored gallery on Sunday evenings. Mr. Smith, a deacon, believed salvation improved workmanship. William sat in the back pew, hymnal upside down to hide his reading. The preacher, a freedman named Reverend Josiah Brown, slipped him a note after service: *"Proverbs 22:1 – A good name is rather to be chosen than great riches."* William memorized the verse, then carved it into a scrap of cedar: *W.C. & E.C. – a good name.*

Ellen, barred from church by the mistress's whims, received her own communion. Ruth Pike began leaving coded messages in the sewing basket: a blue thread meant *safe*, red meant *danger*. In April, a blue thread arrived with a scrap of newspaper: *"Railroad excursion to Savannah, December 21, $5 round trip."* Ellen's pulse raced. She stitched the date into the hem of the green coat—tiny, invisible crosses.

By summer 1848, the disguises were nearly complete. Ellen had added a cravat, a waistcoat, a pair of boots stuffed with paper to enlarge her feet. William had fashioned a small traveling case from scrap mahogany, its false bottom perfect for hiding papers. Their courtship was conducted in absences: a glimpse at the market, a shadow passing the Big House gate, a message carved or stitched.

On August 15, 1848, William delivered a wardrobe to the Collins residence. Ellen met him at the back door, a bundle of linens in her arms. For thirty seconds, they stood in the pantry's dim light. No embrace—too risky. Instead, William pressed the cedar scrap into her hand: *W.C. & E.C.* Ellen slipped the green broadcloth band around his wrist, tying it with a knot only she could undo.

"December twenty-first," she whispered. "Four o'clock train," he answered. Then the cook's footsteps echoed, and they parted—master's property returning to their cages, hearts beating in synchrony.

The ledger still valued William at $1,500, Ellen at $1,200. But in the loft and the attic, a new accounting had begun: one coat, one sling, one heart divided by distance, multiplied by resolve.

Macon, December 1848 – The Final Cut

December 1848 arrived in Macon like a held breath. Frost silvered the cotton fields; the Ocmulgee River ran slow and black under a low sky. In the cabinet shop, the pace had slackened—orders filled, accounts settled, the white apprentices drunk on peach brandy and holiday leave. Mr. Smith locked the tool crib early, muttering about sermons and eggnog. William Craft had never been more alone, or more alive.

He spent the evenings in the loft, the brass key now superfluous; the duplicate had opened every drawer, every secret. From the false bottom of his mahogany case he withdrew the accumulations of two years: train schedules copied in Tommy Pike's spidled hand, a map inked on brown paper, $8.75 in coins earned from odd repairs and hidden in a hollowed chisel handle. He counted the money by candlelight, stacking the coins in towers of possibility. *Cabin to Savannah: $6. Steamer to Charleston: $5. From there...* The numbers blurred. He rubbed his eyes, then added a final entry to his sandpaper ledger: *Freedom: priceless.*

On December 19, he made his boldest move. Mr. Smith, deep in his cups, had left the shop's account book open on the desk. William slipped downstairs, heart hammering against his ribs like a mallet on oak. With a goose-quill pen he forged a pass:

Permit bearer, William Craft, cabinetmaker, to travel to Savannah on business for I. H. Smith. Return by 25th inst. Signed, I. H. Smith.

The signature was a creditable mimicry—practiced on scraps for months. He blotted the ink, folded the paper small, and tucked it inside the cedar scrap with the carved initials. A forgery, yes. But the first document he had ever authored that declared him a man with purpose.

Across town, Ellen Craft worked with the precision of a watchmaker. The mistress had retreated to her bed with laudanum and complaints; the Big House was hushed, the other slaves given leave to visit kin. Ellen had the attic to herself. On the night of December 20, she laid out the disguise on the cedar chest like a surgeon's instruments: the bottle-green coat, the sling, the cravat, the boots, the spectacles. She tried the ensemble before the cracked mirror, adjusting the sling to hide her right hand, practicing the cough that would excuse her illiteracy.

She had added one final touch: a small leather pouch sewn inside the coat's lining, containing $3.50 in coins—saved from selling eggs the mistress never missed—and a lock of her own hair, cut the previous summer. *Evidence,* she thought, echoing William's earlier words. *For the children we'll have.*

At dusk on December 21, she descended to the kitchen. The cook, Aunt Sukey, pressed a parcel into her hands: cornbread, salt pork, a flask of water. "You take care, child," the old woman whispered, eyes wet. Ellen nodded, unable to speak. She slipped out the back door and melted into the shadows of the pecan grove, the green coat bundled beneath her apron.

William waited at the corner of Poplar and Cherry, a shadow among shadows. When Ellen appeared, the moonlight caught the spectacles in her bundle. For a moment they simply looked—two fugitives in plain clothes, the weight of centuries between them. Then William took the bundle, slung it over his shoulder with the mahogany case.

"Four o'clock train," he said. "Mr. William Johnson and valet," she answered. They did not touch. Not yet. The risk was too great.

They walked separately to the depot, William ahead, Ellen trailing by a block. The station was nearly deserted—holiday travelers already gone, drunks asleep on benches. William purchased two tickets with the forged pass: cabin for the "gentleman," steerage for the "servant." The clerk barely glanced up.

At 3:47 a.m., the train whistle split the night. William boarded first, taking a seat in the colored car. Ellen followed minutes later, transformed. The coat hung loose on her narrow frame; the sling concealed her hand; the spectacles masked her eyes. She moved with the stiff gait of an invalid, coughing into the linen. A white passenger offered his seat. She accepted with a gruff "Much obliged," her voice pitched low, the Georgia lilt softened to a planter's drawl.

William watched from the doorway between cars, his heart a drumbeat. When the train lurched forward, Macon's lights receding into the dark, he allowed himself one breath of exultation. The cabinetmaker and the seamstress, apprentice and house girl, were no longer property. They were passengers on a journey measured in miles and minutes, with freedom as the destination.

In the loft, the sandpaper ledger lay open to its final entry, written in William's steady hand:

December 21, 1848 – Departed Macon. Destination: Philadelphia. Cost: one coat, one sling, two lives. Paid in full.

In the attic, the primer remained beneath the floorboard, open to the page where Ellen had written: *The Crafts will sit free.* Beside it, in fresh ink: *And they did.*

The train gathered speed, iron wheels singing on iron rails. Somewhere between the click of the ties, William and Ellen Craft crossed an invisible threshold. The cabinet shop and the Big House shrank to memories, the ledger and the cedar chest to relics. Ahead lay 1,000 miles of daylight, and a love that had apprenticed itself to liberty.

Three

CHAPTER 3 A Marriage in Secret

The Woods Beyond Mulberry Street – June 1846

The pine forest west of Macon began where the cotton fields surrendered to scrub and shadow. In June 1846, the air beneath the canopy hung heavy with resin and the low thrum of insects, a green cathedral untouched by overseer's bell or master's ledger. It was here, on the evening of the summer solstice, that William and Ellen Craft stepped beyond the boundaries of bondage to forge a covenant no law could recognize.

They had met only thrice since the auction—once at the parade, once in the pantry, once when William delivered a repaired cradle and Ellen accepted it with a whispered *"Sunday."* The word had been enough. Sunday, June 21, was slave visiting day; passes were lax, patrols sparse. William left the cabinet shop at dusk with a bundle of tools slung over his shoulder—ostensibly to repair a neighbor's gate. Ellen slipped out the Big House kitchen door with a basket of mending, Aunt Sukey's knowing nod her only witness.

They converged at the forest's edge, two figures swallowed by twilight. William wore his Sunday osnaburg, cleaned and pressed; Ellen, a faded gingham dress, her hair braided tight to keep the burrs at bay. Neither spoke until the path narrowed and the lights of Macon faded behind the trees.

William led her to a clearing ringed by loblolly pines, where a fallen log formed a natural altar. He had prepared the space with the precision of a cabinetmaker: the log swept clean of moss, a circle of river stones at its base, a single dogwood blossom placed like a vow. In the center lay the cedar scrap with their initials, now polished smooth and threaded with a strip of green broadcloth—Ellen's signal band, returned.

Ellen's breath caught. "You did this," she said, not a question. "With my own hands," William answered. "Like everything worth keeping."

They knelt on the pine needles. The forest held its breath. William produced a small Bible—borrowed from Reverend Josiah Brown's church gallery, its leather cover cracked but its pages intact. He opened to Ruth 1:16, the verse he had memorized by lantern light: *"Entreat me not to leave thee..."* His voice, steady from years of reading bills of sale, trembled only slightly.

Ellen placed her hand atop his. "I have no ring," she said. "Nor I," he replied. "But I have this." He lifted the cedar scrap, the green thread now tied in a lover's knot. "Where you go, I go. Where you lodge, I lodge. Your people shall be my people, and your God my God."

She echoed the words, her voice clear as spring water. "Where you die, I will die, and there will I be buried. The Lord do so to me, and more also, if aught but death part thee and me."

They bound their hands with the green thread, the knot tight but not cruel. William spoke next, improvising from the marrow of his bones: "I take you, Ellen, as my wife in the sight of God and these pines. No chain can hold what love has joined."

Ellen's eyes shone. "I take you, William, as my husband. In sickness and in health, in bondage and—" her voice caught, then steadied—"in whatever lies beyond."

They leaned forward. The kiss was brief, chaste, sealed with the taste of pine sap and possibility. When they parted, the dogwood blossom had fallen between them, its petals bruised but intact.

William broke the silence. "We cannot stay." "I know," Ellen said. "But we have this."

They stood. The forest had grown darker; an owl called once, then fell silent. William tucked the cedar scrap into Ellen's palm. "Keep it close. When the time comes, it will be our compass."

Ellen pressed it to her heart. "And when we are free, we will carve our names in something that lasts."

They walked back separately—William first, Ellen ten minutes behind. At the forest's edge, she paused beneath a slash pine and whispered to the night: *"Where you go, I go."* The words were a vow, a map, a seed.

Oral histories from the Woodville descendants—preserved in interviews conducted by the Federal Writers' Project in 1937—recall Ellen speaking of that night decades later: *"We was married in the woods, with the trees for witnesses and the stars for candles. No preacher, no paper, but the Lord knew, and so did we."*

In the Big House, Ellen hid the cedar scrap beneath her pallet, wrapped in the primer. In the loft, William carved a second knot into his pallet post—two strands intertwined, unbreakable. The marriage was illegal, the ceremony unsanctioned, but the bond was forged in the only court that mattered: their own.

The first escape fantasy was born that night, not as a plan but as a promise. As William lay in the loft, listening to the distant train whistle, he imagined a future where the green thread became a wedding ring, where the cedar scrap became a headboard carved with their children's names. Ellen, in the attic, traced the initials by moonlight and dreamed of a porch in Philadelphia, a table made by William's hands, a life measured in years rather than dollars.

The woods kept their secret. The pines stood sentinel. And somewhere between the rustle of leaves and the hush of night, William and Ellen Craft became husband and wife.

Macon, July–December 1846 – Living the Vow, Birthing the Plan

The summer of 1846 burned itself into memory with heat, secrecy, and the first fragile blueprint of escape. William and Ellen Craft were now husband and wife in the eyes of God and the pines, but to Macon they remained Dr. Collins's cabinetmaker and Mrs. Collins's house girl—property valued at $2,700 combined, their union as invisible as the green thread knotted beneath Ellen's chemise.

They met only in stolen increments: a glance across the market square, a whispered phrase passed through Aunt Sukey, a Sunday evening when

CHAPTER 3 A Marriage in Secret

William "delivered" a mended chair and Ellen "received" it at the back door. Each encounter was a risk measured in heartbeats. The patrols had doubled since a failed escape in nearby Clinton; the lash was quick, the auction block quicker. Yet the vow—*Where you go, I go*—became their private liturgy, repeated in silence whenever distance threatened to fracture them.

July brought the first test. Dr. Collins decided to hire William out to a Savannah cabinetmaker for the fall season—$200 for three months, a tidy profit. The news reached William via Mr. Smith's ledger, open on the desk like a death sentence. That night he climbed to the loft, the cedar scrap clenched in his fist. He carved a single word beneath the intertwined knot: *NO*. Then he did what he had never done before: he prayed aloud, the words tumbling into the dark like shavings from a plane. *"Let me stay. Let us stay together."*

The prayer was answered, indirectly. A yellow-fever scare swept the coast; Savannah's docks closed, the hire canceled. William remained in Macon, the ledger entry crossed out in red ink. He took it as a sign. The following Sunday, he pressed a tiny chisel into Ellen's palm during their three-second pantry exchange. *For the locks we'll need to pick,* he mouthed. She tucked it into her primer beside the cedar scrap.

Ellen's days were a gauntlet of servitude and subterfuge. The mistress, heavy with child, demanded constant attendance; Ellen rose at four, scrubbed floors, laid fires, stitched layettes until her fingers bled. But the attic remained her sanctuary. There, by candle stubs pilfered from the dining room, she expanded her map. She added steamer routes from Savannah to Charleston, calculated fares in the margins: *Cabin, $6; deck passage, $3.* She practiced her gentleman's cough until it rattled convincingly, rehearsed excuses for illiteracy: *"Rheumatism in the writing hand, sir."*

In August, Ruth Pike—Tommy's abolitionist sister—became their unwitting courier. She delivered a bolt of broadcloth to the Big House and, with it, a folded note hidden in the selvage: *"December 21—excursion train to Savannah, $5 round trip. Cabin empty."* Ruth's eyes met Ellen's for a fraction of a second: *I know.* Ellen burned the note in the kitchen stove, but the date seared itself into her mind.

September's heat broke with thunderstorms that turned Macon's streets to red mud. William used the chaos to his advantage. During a deluge, he "repaired" the depot's ticket window ledge, lingering long enough to memorize the clerk's routine: tickets sold until 6 p.m., passenger lists posted at noon, no questions for white gentlemen with "servants." He carved the schedule into the mahogany case's false bottom: *Depart 4 a.m., arrive Savannah 2 p.m.*

October brought the first overt danger. Jedediah, the surly apprentice, discovered William's sandpaper ledger beneath the loft floorboard. He waved it like a trophy. "Lookee here—nigger's keepin' books!" Mr. Smith, hungover and irritable, confiscated the scraps but—crucially—did not search further. The cedar scrap, the chisel, the coins remained hidden. That night William moved his cache to the chimney's soot-blackened interior, reachable only by standing on the loft's highest crate.

Ellen faced her own crucible. The mistress, suspecting pilfered laudanum, ordered a search of the servants' quarters. Ellen's heart stopped as the overseer's wife rifled her pallet. The primer, the cedar scrap, the chisel— all were in the attic, safe. But the close call crystallized the timeline. *We leave this year,* she wrote in the primer's margin, *or we are lost.*

November's chill sharpened their resolve. They met twice in the woods— the same clearing, now carpeted with fallen pine needles. The first meeting lasted seven minutes. William brought a new forgery: a doctor's certificate attesting to "Mr. William Johnson's" rheumatic fever, excusing signature. Ellen brought the completed sling, padded to hide her hand. They practiced the roles: "Valet, fetch my portmanteau." "Yes, sir, directly." The words felt like armor.

The second meeting, on November 29, was their wedding night in earnest. Beneath a hunter's moon, they lay on William's spread coat, the cedar scrap between them. No preacher, no witnesses, but the consummation was tender, urgent, a sealing of the vow. Afterward, Ellen traced the scar on William's wrist—an old shackle mark—and whispered, "This will be the last chain you wear." William kissed the callus on her sewing finger. "And this the last you bleed for them."

CHAPTER 3 *A Marriage in Secret*

December arrived with holiday laxity. Passes were granted freely; patrols drank sorghum whiskey. On December 20, Ellen received her final privilege: permission to visit Aunt Sukey's cabin on Christmas Eve. She used the time to pack the disguise in a flour sack, the cedar scrap sewn into the hem. William spent the day forging a second pass—this one for Ellen as "Mr. Johnson's body servant." He signed it with a flourish: *I. H. Smith.*

Oral histories from Woodville descendants, recorded in 1937, preserve Ellen's recollection: *"We didn't have a honeymoon, 'cept the woods and the moon. But we had a plan, and that was better than any ring."*

On December 21, as Macon slept off its Christmas feasting, William and Ellen Craft walked separately to the depot. The vow spoken in June—*Where you go, I go*—had become a timetable, a disguise, a one-way ticket north. The escape fantasy, born in a pine clearing, had hardened into strategy. The secret marriage, illegal under Georgia law, was now the engine of their liberty.

The train whistle sounded at 3:55 a.m. William boarded the colored car, heart pounding. Ellen followed as Mr. William Johnson, Esquire, coughing into her sling. As the locomotive lurched forward, the green thread around William's wrist—tied by Ellen months earlier—caught the lantern light. He touched it once, a silent renewal of the vow.

Behind them, Macon receded into the dark. Ahead lay 1,000 miles of daylight, and a marriage no law could sunder.

Part Two

THE 1,000-MILE GAMBLE

Four

Mr. William Johnson & Valet

Macon Depot – 3:30 a.m. to 4:15 a.m., 21 December 1848

Macon & Western depot crouched at the edge of town like a sleeping iron beast, its platform lit by a single oil lamp that hissed and spat in the pre-dawn chill. Frost glittered on the rails; the air carried the bite of coal smoke and the faint, sweet rot of the Ocmulgee. At 3:30 a.m. on December 21, 1848, the station was nearly deserted—only a yawning porter sweeping ticket stubs, a drunk curled beneath a bench, and the ticket clerk, Mr. Absalom Greer, warming his hands over a tin of coals.

William Craft arrived first, a shadow in osnaburg and wool cap, the mahogany traveling case slung across his shoulder. He had walked the three miles from Poplar Street in silence, rehearsing the forged pass in his pocket: *Permit bearer to Savannah on business.* His pulse kept time with his footsteps—steady, deliberate, the rhythm of a man who had planed a thousand boards to perfection. He took position behind a stack of cotton bales, eyes fixed on the depot door.

Ellen Craft—Mr. William Johnson, Esquire—arrived at 3:42, moving with the stiff gait of an invalid. The bottle-green broadcloth coat hung loose on her narrow frame; the white linen sling cradled her right arm; the green-tinted spectacles masked her eyes. A beaver top hat, purchased from a peddler for fifty cents, sat low over her cropped hair. She coughed into the sling—a wet, convincing rattle practiced for months in the attic. The porter glanced up, then away; white gentlemen with ailments were beneath notice.

William watched from the shadows as Ellen approached the ticket window. Every detail had been drilled: *Lean on the cane. Cough on the third step. Speak in a low drawl.* The cane—borrowed from the mistress's late father—tapped the platform like a metronome. Ellen's heart hammered so fiercely she feared Greer could hear it, but her face remained a mask of planter's ennui.

Greer looked up, bleary-eyed. "Mornin', sir. Savannah?" Ellen nodded, coughing again. "Cabin passage. One gentleman, one servant." Her voice was gravel and honey—low, authoritative, the accent of a lowcountry planter softened by illness.

Greer slid the ticket ledger forward. "Name and signature, sir. And the servant's pass."

Ellen's stomach lurched. The moment of truth. She extended her left hand—the ungloved one—and took the pen with deliberate slowness. "Rheumatism," she rasped, tapping the sling. "Can't write a lick. My man'll sign for me."

William stepped from the shadows, hat in hand, the picture of deference. "William Craft, sir. Body servant to Mr. William Johnson of Augusta." He produced both passes—the forged one for himself, the second for Ellen as "gentleman." Greer barely glanced at them; white invalids with literate slaves were common enough.

"Six dollars cabin, three-fifty steerage," Greer muttered. William counted out the coins—nine dollars and fifty cents, every cent earned and hidden over two years. Greer scribbled the tickets, tore them from the book, and slid them across. "Train boards at four. Colored car's rear."

Ellen accepted the tickets with her left hand, tucking them into her waistcoat. "Much obliged," she said, coughing again for good measure. She turned away, cane tapping, and William fell in behind her—three paces back, eyes down, the perfect valet.

They moved to the platform's far end, where the lamp's glow barely reached. William set the mahogany case beside a bench. For the first time since the woods, they were alone together in public. Ellen sat, arranging the coat to hide her trembling knees. William stood, ostensibly guarding the luggage, but his eyes never left her.

"You were perfect," he whispered. "So were you," she answered, the planter's drawl gone, her own voice soft and fierce. "We're on the train."

The depot clock struck 3:55. The distant whistle sounded—first a low moan, then a shriek that split the night. The iron beast stirred. Porters shouted; the drunk on the bench groaned. Ellen adjusted her spectacles, took a final breath of Georgia air, and became Mr. William Johnson completely.

At 4:00 a.m., the train pulled in—engine No. 17, the *Savannah Express*, its cars painted crimson and gold, windows glowing like eyes. Steam billowed; sparks flew. The conductor, a burly man named Captain Rufus Beall, swung down with a lantern. "All aboard!" he bellowed. "Cabin passengers to the front!"

Ellen rose, cane tapping, and boarded the first-class car. William followed with the case, taking his place in the colored section at the rear. The door slammed. The bell rang. At 4:07 a.m., the train lurched forward, wheels screeching on frost-slick rails.

Macon receded into the dark. The depot lamp shrank to a pinprick, then vanished. Ellen sat by the window, the sling cradling her "invalid" arm, the green spectacles reflecting the passing pines. William, three cars back, touched the green thread at his wrist and smiled into the darkness.

The first test was passed. The ticket clerk had not questioned the gentleman who could not write, the valet who could. Nine dollars and fifty cents had bought them 190 miles of daylight. But the journey had only begun.

Savannah Wharf – 1:45 p.m. to 3:30 p.m., 21 December 1848

The *Savannah Express* hissed into the Savannah depot at 1:47 p.m., right on the printed schedule William had memorized. Steam clouded the platform; the smell of brine and tar replaced the pine of middle Georgia. Passengers spilled out—planters in frock coats, ladies with parasols, slaves balancing trunks on their heads. Ellen Craft—Mr. William Johnson, Esquire—descended the steps of the cabin car with the deliberate slowness of a man twice her age. The cane tapped; the sling cradled; the cough rattled. No one looked twice.

William followed, the mahogany case balanced on one shoulder, eyes scanning for threats. The depot swarmed with uniforms: city constables, customs officers, and the ever-present slave-catchers lounging against cotton bales. A notice board bore fresh handbills—*RUNAWAY: JIM, 25, scar on left cheek, $200 reward*—but none for a light-skinned gentleman and his valet. Yet.

They had ninety minutes before the Charleston steamer, the *General Clinch*, cast off at 3:00 p.m. William had studied the wharf layout from a broadside Tommy Pike had smuggled: *Dock 3, cabin tickets at the purser's office, colored passengers aft.* The plan was simple: secure passage, board early, avoid conversation. Simple, but not safe.

Ellen led the way, cane tapping across the cobblestones toward the waterfront. The Savannah River stretched wide and brown, choked with schooners, flatboats, and the *Clinch* herself—three decks, twin smokestacks, paddlewheels churning even at rest. Gulls wheeled overhead; the air tasted of salt and fish. Ellen's spectacles fogged in the humidity; she wiped them with her free hand, careful not to dislodge the hat.

At the purser's office—a wooden shack with a tin roof—Ellen took her place in line behind a rice planter and his wife. William stood three paces back, head bowed, the perfect servant. The planter glanced at the "gentleman" with the sling, then away. Ellen's heart pounded so loudly she feared the purser could hear it.

The purser, a thin man named Mr. Hiram Dodd, wore a green eyeshade and a scowl. "Name?" he barked. "William Johnson, Esquire, of Augusta," Ellen answered, the drawl thicker now, laced with Charleston vowels. "Cabin passage to Charleston. Myself and my man."

Dodd slid the ledger forward. "Sign here. And the servant's pass."

Ellen coughed—a deep, wet hack that turned heads. "Rheumatism," she rasped, tapping the sling. "Can't hold a pen. My man'll sign."

William stepped forward, producing the forged passes. Dodd squinted at the signatures—*I. H. Smith* in William's careful mimicry—then at William's face. For a heartbeat, time froze. Dodd's eyes narrowed; he had seen hundreds of passes, knew the smell of fresh ink. William's pulse thundered, but his face remained blank.

Mr. William Johnson & Valet

"Augusta, eh?" Dodd said. "You know Colonel Habersham?" Ellen leaned on the cane, coughing again. "Intimately," she croaked. "He'll vouch for me when we dock."

Dodd hesitated, then shrugged. White gentlemen with ailments were not his concern. "Eleven dollars cabin, five steerage," he muttered. William counted out the coins—sixteen dollars total, every cent scraped from odd jobs and hidden in the chisel handle. Dodd scribbled the tickets, tore them from the book, and waved them on.

They moved toward the gangplank. The *Clinch* loomed above, its decks alive with activity. Cabin passengers boarded first; Ellen ascended the forward gangway, cane tapping each step. William followed with the case, directed aft to the colored section. A deckhand—black, free papers in his pocket—glanced at William's pass and nodded him through.

At 2:15 p.m., they were aboard. Ellen took a seat in the saloon, a mahogany-paneled room with velvet settees and brass spittoons. She arranged herself by a window, the sling concealing her hand, the spectacles hiding her eyes. William stowed the case in the colored hold, then took position near the saloon door—close enough to signal, far enough to pass as attendant.

The captain, Josiah Lawton, made his rounds at 2:30. A tall man with a beard like Spanish moss, he paused at Ellen's seat. "Mr. Johnson, is it? You travel light for a gentleman."

Ellen coughed, a performance honed in the attic. "Business in Charleston," she rasped. "My man carries all I need."

Lawton's eyes flicked to the sling, then to William. "Your servant—he's literate?" "Taught him figures for the plantation books," Ellen lied smoothly. "Saves me the trouble."

Lawton grunted, unconvinced but uninterested. White invalids with clever slaves were common enough. He moved on.

At 2:45, the whistle blew. The paddlewheels churned; the *Clinch* eased from the dock. Savannah's wharves receded, replaced by marsh and river. Ellen watched the shoreline through the window, her reflection in the glass a stranger's: top hat, green spectacles, the face of a man who belonged. William, from the doorway, caught her eye and gave the smallest nod. *We're clear.*

The second test was passed. The purser had not questioned the passes; the captain had not pressed. Sixteen dollars had bought them 200 miles of water. But Charleston loomed, and with it, new dangers.

Charleston Harbor & Saloon – 6:00 a.m. to 8:30 p.m., 22 December 1848

The *General Clinch* nosed into Charleston harbor at dawn, her paddlewheels churning the Cooper River into frothy lace. The city rose before them: church spires piercing a rose-gold sky, wharves bristling with masts, the air thick with salt and the clamor of a port that never slept. Ellen Craft—Mr. William Johnson—stood at the saloon window, spectacles fogged by the steam of her own breath. The sling hid her trembling right hand; the cane rested against her knee like a faithful dog. Ten hours on the water had passed without incident, but Charleston was a crucible.

William had spent the night in the colored hold, wedged between cotton bales and snoring deckhands. He had not slept. Every creak of the hull, every shout from the deck, had been a potential alarm. At 5:30 a.m., he had slipped topside to check the schedule posted near the purser's cabin: *Arrive Charleston 6:00 a.m.; depart for Wilmington 9:00 p.m. via rail.* Fifteen hours in the city—too long, too exposed. The plan was to board the evening train immediately, but tickets required another encounter with authority.

At 6:15, the gangplank thudded down. Cabin passengers disembarked first. Ellen descended with the stiff gait of her invalid persona, coughing into the sling as dockhands stared. William followed with the mahogany case, eyes scanning for constables. The wharf teemed: porters in red caps, factors in silk hats, slaves unloading rice barrels. A handbill fluttered on a post—*RUNAWAY: LUCY, 18, speaks French, $300 reward*—but none for a gentleman and valet.

They had arranged to kill time in the Charleston Hotel's public parlor—neutral ground, open to white travelers. Ellen led the way up Meeting Street, cane tapping cobblestones still slick with dew. The hotel's white columns gleamed; a liveried doorman bowed her through. Inside, the parlor smelled of coffee and beeswax. Ellen took a corner table, ordering tea with her left hand. William stood behind her chair, the perfect attendant.

At 7:00 a.m., the breakfast bell rang. The dining room filled with planters, merchants, and a Prussian naval officer in braid. Ellen hesitated—food meant conversation—but hunger won. She entered, William trailing. The maître d' seated "Mr. Johnson" at a table near the window, William standing at parade rest.

The trap sprang at 7:30.

A burly man in a brocade waistcoat—Mr. Enoch Grooms, a Macon slave trader known to both Crafts—strode in with two companions. Grooms had sold William's brother two years prior; he had bid on Ellen at the 1846 auction. His eyes swept the room and locked on the "gentleman" with the sling.

"Well, bless my soul!" Grooms boomed, crossing the floor. "If it ain't young Johnson from Augusta! Your daddy's old friend, Enoch Grooms—don't you recall me from the Macon races?"

Ellen's blood turned to ice. She coughed violently, buying time. "Rheumatism's got my memory, sir," she rasped. "And my voice."

Grooms pulled out a chair uninvited. "Nonsense! Sit, sit. Your man can fetch coffee." He snapped at William. "Boy, jump!"

William moved with mechanical obedience, but his eyes flicked to Ellen: *Stall.* He returned with a silver pot, pouring with exaggerated care. Grooms leaned in, peering at the sling. "Heard your daddy sold that fancy girl of his—light-skinned wench, name of Ellen. Shame. She'd fetch two thousand in New Orleans."

Ellen's teacup rattled. She coughed again, spilling tea on the cloth. "Apologies," she croaked. "Fever's on me."

Grooms waved it off. "No matter. Tell me, Johnson—why travel with just one nigger? Prime stock like yours ought to have a retinue."

Ellen seized the opening. "The rest took sick. Yellow fever. Left 'em in Augusta." She gestured weakly at William. "This one's all I trust with my medicine."

Grooms squinted at William, then at the sling. Recognition flickered—then died. The disguise, the context, the authority of whiteness held. "Well," he grunted, "mind the Charleston market. Prime bucks going for eighteen hundred."

The Prussian officer at the next table laughed. "In Hamburg, we pay sailors, not own them!" The room tittered. Grooms flushed, distracted. Ellen seized the moment. "My man'll settle the bill," she said, rising. "Business calls."

She limped out, William behind her. In the lobby, she collapsed onto a settee, spectacles askew. "He knew us," she whispered. "But he didn't," William answered. "We're ghosts in daylight."

They had three hours until the train. Ellen bought tickets with shaking hands—$12 for cabin to Wilmington, $6 for William. The clerk never looked up. At 8:45 p.m., they boarded the Charleston & Wilmington Railroad, Ellen in the first-class car, William aft. As the train pulled out, the city's lights blurred into streaks of gold.

The third test was passed. The slave trader had sat inches away and seen only a sickly planter and his valet. Twelve dollars had bought them 140 miles of rail. But the night was young, and the border loomed.

Wilmington to Philadelphia – Midnight, 22 December to Dawn, 25 December 1848

The Charleston & Wilmington train clattered north through pine barrens and marsh, its rhythm a metallic lullaby. Ellen Craft—Mr. William Johnson—sat rigid in the first-class car, sling cradling her "rheumatic" arm, green spectacles reflecting the oil-lamp glow. The encounter with Enoch Grooms had drained her; every cough now felt like a confession. Across the aisle, a Methodist minister snored; beside her, a Richmond merchant read the *Charleston Mercury* by candle stub. William, three cars back in the colored section, clutched the mahogany case and counted mileposts in the dark.

At 11:47 p.m., the train jerked to a halt in Wilmington, North Carolina. Lanterns swung; conductors shouted. Ellen's stomach knotted. Wilmington was a slave port; patrols were thick. The plan was to change trains for Richmond, then another for Washington, then Philadelphia—four legs, four borders. But the schedule had slipped; the Richmond connection was delayed until 2:00 a.m. Two hours exposed on a platform crawling with constables.

Ellen descended with the other cabin passengers, cane tapping, cough rattling. William followed, eyes scanning. A handbill on the depot wall read: *VIGILANCE—ALL PASSES INSPECTED*. A deputy in a slouch hat paced the platform, lantern raised. Ellen's heart hammered. She limped toward the waiting room, William trailing.

Inside, a fire crackled. Ellen took a bench near the stove, arranging herself like a man too ill for scrutiny. William stood behind her, ostensibly guarding the case. The deputy entered, lantern swinging. "Passes!" he barked.

White passengers produced papers; Ellen extended her left hand, the forged doctor's certificate trembling slightly. The deputy squinted at the sling, then at William's pass. "This your boy?" "My valet," Ellen rasped. "Loyal as they come."

The deputy grunted, moving on. Ellen exhaled silently. *Test four: passed.*

At 2:15 a.m., the Richmond train—a rattling string of wooden cars—pulled in. Ellen boarded the cabin section; William, the colored. The train lurched north, crossing the Cape Fear River into the Carolina night. Ellen dozed fitfully, dreaming of Macon's auction block. William stayed awake, carving a tiny notch into the case for every mile.

Dawn broke gray over Petersburg, Virginia. At 6:00 a.m., they changed for the Richmond, Fredericksburg & Potomac line. Ellen's cough was no longer acting; exhaustion and cold had settled in her chest. In Richmond, a new danger: the train to Aquia Creek required a ferry across the Potomac, and Virginia law mandated inspection of all colored passengers.

At the Richmond depot, a U.S. marshal boarded with a clipboard. "Free papers or passes!" he demanded. William produced the forged documents; the marshal's eyes narrowed. "This boy literate?" "Taught him figures for the plantation," Ellen croaked from the doorway, swaying on her cane. "Saves me trouble."

The marshal hesitated, then waved them through. *Test five: passed.*

The ferry to Aquia Creek was a flatboat under a leaden sky. Ellen stood on deck, wind whipping her coat, the Potomac's chop mirroring her nerves. William, below with the luggage, touched the green thread at his wrist. *Where you go, I go.*

At Aquia Creek, the final train—the Washington & Philadelphia—waited. Ellen boarded the parlor car, velvet seats and chandeliers a mockery of her terror. William took the colored bench. The conductor, a kindly Quaker named Mr. Harlan, checked tickets. "Philadelphia, sir?" he asked Ellen. "God willing," she rasped.

DISGUISED IN DAYLIGHT

At 3:00 p.m., December 24, the train crossed the Mason-Dixon Line. Ellen felt it in her bones before the conductor announced it. Maryland's slave pens gave way to Pennsylvania's farms. She removed the spectacles, blinking at the light. William, sensing the shift, smiled from the doorway.

The final crisis came at the Pennsylvania border. A customs officer boarded at Havre de Grace, demanding signatures for baggage. Ellen coughed, extending the sling. "Rheumatism," she whispered. The officer, harried by holiday travelers, waved her through. William signed with a flourish. *Test six: passed.*

At 4:17 a.m., Christmas Dawn, 1848, the train steamed into Philadelphia's Broad Street Station. Snow fell soft and silent, blanketing the city in white. Ellen descended, legs trembling, cane forgotten in the car. William followed, the mahogany case light as freedom.

They stood on the platform, two fugitives in broad daylight. Ellen looked at William, tears freezing on her lashes. "We're here," she said, voice breaking. "Where you go, I go," he answered, and for the first time, they embraced in public—husband and wife, free.

Abolitionist William Still waited with a carriage, alerted by a coded telegram from Charleston. "Welcome to liberty," he said, eyes wide at the disguise. Ellen laughed—a sound like church bells. William touched the cedar scrap in her pocket, the green thread at his wrist. The ledger was closed. The journey—1,000 miles, six tests, four days—was complete.

Philadelphia's snow kept falling, erasing their footprints. Behind them, Georgia's chains lay buried. Ahead, a new life, carved by love and courage, began.

Five

Savannah: The Captain's Doubt

Savannah Wharf – 1:47 p.m. to 2:45 p.m., 21 December 1848

The *Savannah Express* hissed into the Savannah depot at 1:47 p.m., its iron wheels screeching against the rails like a warning. Steam billowed across the platform, mingling with the salt-heavy air of the riverfront. Ellen Craft—Mr. William Johnson, Esquire—descended the cabin car steps with the calculated frailty of a consumptive planter. The bottle-green broadcloth coat hung loose on her frame; the white linen sling cradled her right arm; the green-tinted spectacles masked eyes that had not closed in twenty-four hours. Each tap of the cane on the wooden planks was a metronome counting down to the next peril.

William followed three paces behind, the mahogany traveling case balanced on his shoulder, his osnaburg shirt damp with sweat despite the December chill. His pulse thrummed in his ears, louder than the gulls wheeling overhead. They had cleared the Macon ticket clerk, but Savannah was a slave-trading hub—wharves crawling with constables, factors, and captains who knew every trick of runaways. One wrong glance, one suspicious question, and the journey would end in irons.

The plan was precise: secure cabin passage on the *General Clinch*, a 300-ton sidewheel steamer bound for Charleston at 3:00 p.m. William had memorized the schedule from a broadside Tommy Pike had smuggled in October: *Dock 3, purser's office open till 2:50, cabin fares $11, colored steerage $5.* They had ninety minutes to cross the wharf, buy tickets, and board—ninety minutes to convince the world that a light-skinned "gentleman" with a bandaged arm and a literate "valet" belonged on a first-class deck.

Ellen led the way, cane tapping across the cobblestones toward the waterfront. The Savannah River stretched wide and brown, choked with schooners, flatboats, and the *Clinch* herself—three decks of white paint and polished brass, her twin smokestacks belching smoke even at rest. The wharf teemed with life: porters in red caps heaving cotton bales, factors in silk hats barking orders, slaves unloading rice barrels under the eye of overseers. A handbill fluttered on a post—*RUNAWAY: SAM, 30, branded on cheek, $250 reward*—but none for a planter and his servant. Yet.

At the purser's office—a squat wooden shack with a tin roof—Ellen took her place in line behind a rice planter and his wife. William stood three paces back, head bowed, the mahogany case at his feet. The planter glanced at the "gentleman" with the sling, then away; invalids were beneath notice. Ellen's heart pounded so fiercely she feared the purser could hear it through the broadcloth.

The purser, Mr. Hiram Dodd, was a thin man with a green eyeshade and a scowl etched deep as the river. He had processed a thousand passages and could smell desperation like blood in the water. "Name?" he barked as Ellen reached the window.

"William Johnson, Esquire, of Augusta," Ellen answered, her voice pitched low, the drawl thickened with Charleston vowels and the rasp of illness. "Cabin passage to Charleston. Myself and my man."

Dodd slid the ledger forward, the pen heavy with scrutiny. "Sign here. And the servant's pass."

Ellen's stomach lurched. The moment of truth. She extended her left hand—the ungloved one—and took the pen with deliberate slowness. "Rheumatism," she croaked, tapping the sling. "Can't write a lick. My man'll sign for me."

William stepped forward, producing the forged passes with the calm of a man who had rehearsed this in a cabinet shop loft for months. The ink

Savannah: The Captain's Doubt

was still crisp—*Permit bearer, William Craft, to accompany Mr. W. Johnson to Charleston, return by 25th inst. Signed, I. H. Smith.* Dodd's eyes narrowed; he had seen fresh forgeries before. He leaned closer, peering at the signature, then at William's face.

"Augusta, eh?" Dodd said, his voice sharp as a fishhook. "You know Colonel Habersham? He sails with us regular."

Ellen coughed—a deep, wet hack that turned heads in the line. "Intimately," she rasped, leaning heavily on the cane. "He'll vouch for me in Charleston."

Dodd's gaze flicked to the sling, then back to the pass. "This boy—your servant—he's mighty light-handed with a pen for a field nigger."

Ellen's mind raced. She tilted her head, cupping her left ear as if straining to hear. "Speak up, sir," she said loudly, her voice suddenly querulous. "Deaf in this ear—fever took it last spring." She coughed again, a performance honed in the Big House attic, and swayed as if dizzy. The rice planter's wife clucked in sympathy.

William seized the opening. "Master's hard of hearing, sir," he said, his tone deferential but firm. "I read and write for the plantation books. Saves him the trouble."

Dodd hesitated, his scowl deepening. The *Charleston Mercury* that morning had carried a notice: *Vigilance advised—runaways adopting disguises.* A white gentleman who couldn't write, a slave who could—it smelled wrong. He tapped the ledger, then looked at the clock. The *Clinch's* whistle was due in twenty minutes.

"Your master's deaf, you say?" Dodd pressed. "Let's see him hear this." He slammed the ledger shut with a crack that echoed off the tin roof.

Ellen blinked, feigning confusion. "Eh? What's that?" She cupped her ear again, leaning forward. "You'll have to speak clearer, sir."

William's panic was a living thing, clawing at his ribs, but his face remained stone. He stepped closer, shielding Ellen with the case. "Beg pardon, sir," he said, "but the gentleman's feverish. We'll miss the tide."

Dodd's eyes darted between them. The line behind grew restless; the rice planter cleared his throat. Finally, Dodd shrugged, the universal language of men paid to move passengers, not solve puzzles. "Eleven dollars cabin, five steerage," he muttered, scribbling the tickets. "Board now or swim."

William counted out the coins—sixteen dollars, every cent earned in secret. Dodd tore the tickets from the book and slid them across. Ellen accepted them with her left hand, tucking them into her waistcoat. "Much obliged," she croaked, already turning away.

They moved toward the gangplank, Ellen's cane tapping a retreating rhythm. William's knees threatened to buckle, but he kept pace. The *Clinch* loomed above, her decks alive with activity. The first test of Savannah—the purser's doubt—was passed, but the captain waited.

Gangplank & Deck of the General Clinch – 2:45 p.m. to 3:15 p.m., 21 December 1848

The gangplank of the *General Clinch* rose at a steep angle, slick with river mist and the grease of a thousand boots. Ellen Craft—Mr. William Johnson—paused at its foot, cane planted like a flag, and let out a theatrical cough that rattled up from her boots. A deckhand in a striped shirt glanced down, then away; white invalids were cargo, not conversation. William stood three paces behind, the mahogany case balanced on his shoulder, every muscle coiled to spring if the purser changed his mind.

At the top of the plank stood Captain Josiah Lawton himself—six feet of weathered oak, beard like Spanish moss, eyes the color of storm water. He had commanded the Savannah–Charleston run for twelve years and could read a face the way a pilot reads tide charts. The *Charleston Mercury* lay folded in his coat pocket, its warning about disguised runaways still warm from the printer's ink. Lawton's gaze locked on the "gentleman" with the sling.

"Mr. Johnson, is it?" Lawton's voice cut through the dock noise like a bosun's whistle. "Dodd says you're deaf in one ear and can't write a lick. That true?"

Ellen ascended slowly, each step deliberate, the cane tapping a syncopated rhythm. Halfway up, she cupped her left ear and shouted, "Speak up, Captain! Fever's taken my hearing!" The words carried to the wharf below; a porter snickered. Ellen swayed, clutching the rail with her free hand as if dizzy. William's heart hammered, but he kept his eyes on the planks—*servant's place*.

Lawton's eyes narrowed. He had seen every ruse: women in men's clothes, boys in bonnets, slaves with forged free papers. But a white planter who couldn't sign his name? That was new. He stepped forward, blocking the gangplank's head. "I run a tight ship, sir. No passengers board without my say-so. Let's see that pass again."

William's stomach dropped. He set the case down with a thud that echoed like a gavel and produced the forged document. Lawton snatched it, holding it to the light. The ink was crisp, the signature *I. H. Smith* elegant but not quite right—Smith was a Macon name, and Lawton knew every factor from here to Augusta. He sniffed the paper. Fresh.

Ellen reached the top, breathing hard, and leaned heavily on the cane. "Captain," she rasped, "my man's got the papers. I'm bound for Charleston on urgent business—family estate. Delay'll cost me a thousand dollars." She coughed again, a wet hack that sprayed mist into the air. A lady passenger behind her recoiled, fanning herself with a glove.

Lawton's gaze flicked from the pass to Ellen's face—pale, delicate, the jaw too smooth for a man's. The sling hid the right hand completely; the spectacles obscured the eyes. He leaned in, voice low. "You look mighty young for a planter, Mr. Johnson. And mighty light-skinned for a man with rheumatism."

Ellen's mind raced. She tilted her head, cupping the "deaf" ear. "Eh? Speak louder, sir! Can't hear a blasted thing!" She swayed again, clutching Lawton's sleeve for support. The captain instinctively steadied her—gentleman's reflex—and in that moment, the disguise held. A white man's touch was proof of status.

William stepped forward, voice steady. "Beg pardon, Captain. Master's feverish and hard of hearing. Doctor in Charleston's waiting. We'll keep to the cabin, no trouble."

Lawton hesitated. The *Clinch*'s whistle was due in ten minutes; the tide waited for no man. Behind him, the rice planter from the purser's line cleared his throat. "Let the invalid pass, Captain. Some of us have schedules."

Lawton's pride warred with caution. He thrust the pass back at William. "Cabin 7, starboard side. Your boy bunks aft with the colored crew. Any funny business, and I'll clap you both in irons." He turned away, barking at a deckhand to secure the cargo nets.

Ellen exhaled silently, a tremor running through her legs. She limped across the deck to Cabin 7—a narrow stateroom with a single berth, a washstand, and a porthole filmed with salt. William followed with the case, closing the door behind them. For the first time since Macon, they were alone.

"You were brilliant," William whispered, setting the case down. "So were you," Ellen answered, collapsing onto the berth. She removed the spectacles, revealing eyes red-rimmed with exhaustion. "He smelled the ink."

"But he didn't taste the lie." William touched the green thread at his wrist—their wedding knot. "We're aboard."

At 3:00 p.m., the *Clinch*'s whistle shrieked. The paddlewheels churned; the steamer eased from the dock. Savannah's wharves receded, replaced by marsh and river. Ellen watched through the porthole, her reflection in the glass a stranger's: top hat, sling, the face of a man who had just outrun a captain's doubt.

The second test of Savannah—the gangplank confrontation—was passed. Sixteen dollars and a performance of deafness had bought them 200 miles of water. But Charleston loomed, and with it, the dinner table trap.

Charleston Harbor & Dinner Saloon – 6:00 a.m. to 8:30 p.m., 22 December 1848

The *General Clinch* steamed into Charleston harbor at dawn, her paddlewheels churning the Cooper River into frothy lace. The city rose before them: church spires piercing a rose-gold sky, wharves bristling with masts, the air thick with salt and the clamor of a port that never slept. Ellen Craft—Mr. William Johnson—stood at the porthole of Cabin 7, spectacles fogged by the steam of her own breath. The sling hid her trembling right hand; the cane rested against the berth like a faithful dog. Ten hours on the water had passed without incident, but Charleston was a crucible.

William had spent the night in the colored hold, wedged between cotton bales and snoring deckhands. He had not slept. Every creak of the hull, every shout from the deck, had been a potential alarm. At 5:30 a.m., he had slipped topside to check the schedule posted near the purser's cabin: *Arrive Charleston 6:00 a.m.; depart for Wilmington 9:00 p.m. via rail*. Fifteen hours in the city—too long, too exposed. The plan was to board the evening train immediately, but

Savannah: The Captain's Doubt

tickets required another encounter with authority.

At 6:15, the gangplank thudded down. Cabin passengers disembarked first. Ellen descended with the stiff gait of her invalid persona, coughing into the sling as dockhands stared. William followed with the mahogany case, eyes scanning for constables. The wharf teemed: porters in red caps, factors in silk hats, slaves unloading rice barrels under the eye of overseers. A handbill fluttered on a post—*RUNAWAY: LUCY, 18, speaks French, $300 reward*—but none for a gentleman and valet.

They had arranged to kill time in the Charleston Hotel's public parlor—neutral ground, open to white travelers. Ellen led the way up Meeting Street, cane tapping cobblestones still slick with dew. The hotel's white columns gleamed; a liveried doorman bowed her through. Inside, the parlor smelled of coffee and beeswax. Ellen took a corner table, ordering tea with her left hand. William stood behind her chair, the perfect attendant.

At 7:00 a.m., the breakfast bell rang. The dining room filled with planters, merchants, and a Prussian naval officer in braid. Ellen hesitated—food meant conversation—but hunger won. She entered, William trailing. The maître d' seated "Mr. Johnson" at a table near the window, William standing at parade rest.

The trap sprang at 7:30.

A burly man in a brocade waistcoat—Mr. Enoch Grooms, a Macon slave trader known to both Crafts—strode in with two companions. Grooms had sold William's brother two years prior; he had bid on Ellen at the 1846 auction. His eyes swept the room and locked on the "gentleman" with the sling.

"Well, bless my soul!" Grooms boomed, crossing the floor. "If it ain't young Johnson from Augusta! Your daddy's old friend, Enoch Grooms—don't you recall me from the Macon races?"

Ellen's blood turned to ice. She coughed violently, buying time. "Rheumatism's got my memory, sir," she rasped. "And my voice."

Grooms pulled out a chair uninvited. "Nonsense! Sit, sit. Your man can fetch coffee." He snapped at William. "Boy, jump!"

William moved with mechanical obedience, but his eyes flicked to Ellen: *Stall.* He returned with a silver pot, pouring with exaggerated care. Grooms leaned in, peering at the sling. "Heard your daddy sold that fancy girl of his—light-skinned wench, name of Ellen. Shame. She'd fetch two thousand in New Orleans."

Ellen's teacup rattled. She coughed again, spilling tea on the cloth. "Apologies," she croaked. "Fever's on me."

Grooms waved it off. "No matter. Tell me, Johnson—why travel with just one nigger? Prime stock like yours ought to have a retinue."

Ellen seized the opening. "The rest took sick. Yellow fever. Left 'em in Augusta." She gestured weakly at William. "This one's all I trust with my medicine."

Grooms squinted at William, then at the sling. Recognition flickered—then died. The disguise, the context, the authority of whiteness held. "Well," he grunted, "mind the Charleston market. Prime bucks going for eighteen hundred."

The Prussian officer at the next table laughed. "In Hamburg, we pay sailors, not own them!" The room tittered. Grooms flushed, distracted. Ellen seized the moment. "My man'll settle the bill," she said, rising. "Business calls."

She limped out, William behind her. In the lobby, she collapsed onto a settee, spectacles askew. "He knew us," she whispered. "But he didn't," William answered. "We're ghosts in daylight."

They had three hours until the train. Ellen bought tickets with shaking hands—$12 for cabin to Wilmington, $6 for William. The clerk never looked up. At 8:45 p.m., they boarded the Charleston & Wilmington Railroad, Ellen in the first-class car, William aft. As the train pulled out, the city's lights blurred into streaks of gold.

The third test of Savannah—the dinner table trap—was passed. Twelve dollars and a performance of illness had bought them 140 miles of rail. But the night was young, and the border loomed.

Wilmington to Philadelphia – Midnight, 22 December to Christmas Dawn, 25 December 1848

The Charleston & Wilmington train clattered north through pine barrens and marsh, its rhythm a metallic heartbeat in the dark. Ellen Craft—Mr. William Johnson—sat rigid in the first-class car, sling cradling her "rheumatic"

Savannah: The Captain's Doubt

arm, green spectacles reflecting the oil-lamp glow. The encounter with Enoch Grooms had drained her; every cough now felt like a confession. Across the aisle, a Methodist minister snored; beside her, a Richmond merchant read the *Charleston Mercury* by candle stub. William, three cars back in the colored section, clutched the mahogany case and counted mileposts in the dark.

At 11:47 p.m., the train jerked to a halt in Wilmington, North Carolina. Lanterns swung; conductors shouted. Ellen's stomach knotted. Wilmington was a slave port; patrols were thick. The plan was to change trains for Richmond, then another for Washington, then Philadelphia—four legs, four borders. But the schedule had slipped; the Richmond connection was delayed until 2:00 a.m. Two hours exposed on a platform crawling with constables.

Ellen descended with the other cabin passengers, cane tapping, cough rattling. William followed, eyes scanning. A handbill on the depot wall read: VIGILANCE—ALL PASSES INSPECTED. A deputy in a slouch hat paced the platform, lantern raised. Ellen's heart hammered. She limped toward the waiting room, William trailing.

Inside, a fire crackled. Ellen took a bench near the stove, arranging herself like a man too ill for scrutiny. William stood behind her, ostensibly guarding the case. The deputy entered, lantern swinging. "Passes!"

White passengers produced papers; Ellen extended her left hand, the forged doctor's certificate trembling slightly. The deputy squinted at the sling, then at William's pass. "This your boy?" "My valet," Ellen rasped. "Loyal as they come."

The deputy grunted, moving on. Ellen exhaled silently. *Test four: passed.*

At 2:15 a.m., the Richmond train—a rattling string of wooden cars—pulled in. Ellen boarded the cabin section; William, the colored. The train lurched north, crossing the Cape Fear River into the Carolina night. Ellen dozed fitfully, dreaming of Macon's auction block. William stayed awake, carving a tiny notch into the case for every mile.

Dawn broke gray over Petersburg, Virginia. At 6:00 a.m., they changed for the Richmond, Fredericksburg & Potomac line. Ellen's cough was no longer acting; exhaustion and cold had settled in her chest. In Richmond, a new danger: the train to Aquia Creek required a ferry across the Potomac, and

Virginia law mandated inspection of all colored passengers.

At the Richmond depot, a U.S. marshal boarded with a clipboard. "Free papers or passes!" he demanded. William produced the forged documents; the marshal's eyes narrowed. "This boy literate?" "Taught him figures for the plantation," Ellen croaked from the doorway, swaying on her cane. "Saves me trouble."

The marshal hesitated, then waved them through. *Test five: passed.*

The ferry to Aquia Creek was a flatboat under a leaden sky. Ellen stood on deck, wind whipping her coat, the Potomac's chop mirroring her nerves. William, below with the luggage, touched the green thread at his wrist. *Where you go, I go.*

At Aquia Creek, the final train—the Washington & Philadelphia—waited. Ellen boarded the parlor car, velvet seats and chandeliers a mockery of her terror. William took the colored bench. The conductor, a kindly Quaker named Mr. Harlan, checked tickets. "Philadelphia, sir?" he asked Ellen. "God willing," she rasped.

At 3:00 p.m., December 24, the train crossed the Mason-Dixon Line. Ellen felt it in her bones before the conductor announced it. Maryland's slave pens gave way to Pennsylvania's farms. She removed the spectacles, blinking at the light. William, sensing the shift, smiled from the doorway.

The final crisis came at the Pennsylvania border. A customs officer boarded at Havre de Grace, demanding signatures for baggage. Ellen coughed, extending the sling. "Rheumatism," she whispered. The officer, harried by holiday travelers, waved her through. William signed with a flourish. *Test six: passed.*

At 4:17 a.m., Christmas Dawn, 1848, the train steamed into Philadelphia's Broad Street Station. Snow fell soft and silent, blanketing the city in white. Ellen descended, legs trembling, cane forgotten in the car. William followed, the mahogany case light as freedom.

They stood on the platform, two fugitives in broad daylight. Ellen looked at William, tears freezing on her lashes. "We're here," she said, voice breaking. "Where you go, I go," he answered, and for the first time, they embraced in public—husband and wife, free.

Savannah: The Captain's Doubt

Abolitionist William Still waited with a carriage, alerted by a coded telegram from Charleston. "Welcome to liberty," he said, eyes wide at the disguise. Ellen laughed—a sound like church bells. William touched the cedar scrap in her pocket, the green thread at his wrist. The ledger was closed. The journey—1,000 miles, six tests, four days—was complete.

Philadelphia's snow kept falling, erasing their footprints. Behind them, Georgia's chains lay buried. Ahead, a new life, carved by love and courage, began.

Six

Charleston: The Dinner Table Trap

Charleston Hotel Dining Room – *7:30 a.m., 22 December 1848*
    The Charleston Hotel dining room gleamed with the opulence of a city built on rice and human flesh. Crystal chandeliers dripped light onto white damask tablecloths; silver clinked against porcelain; the air carried coffee, ham, and the faint metallic tang of fear. Ellen Craft—Mr. William Johnson, Esquire—entered at 7:25 a.m., cane tapping a measured cadence across the parquet floor. The bottle-green coat was rumpled from the steamer berth; the sling cradled her right arm like a secret; the green spectacles masked eyes that had seen only four hours of sleep in three days. Each step was a performance, each cough a shield.

William followed three paces behind, the mahogany case balanced on his shoulder, his osnaburg shirt pressed despite the night in the *Clinch*'s colored hold. He had not eaten since Macon, but hunger was a familiar companion. His role was simple: valet, silent, invisible. Yet every nerve screamed vigilance. Charleston was the lion's den—slave pens on every corner, auctions advertised in the *Mercury*, traders who knew Dr. Collins's stock by sight.

The maître d', a freedman named Mr. Lucius Drayton, seated "Mr. Johnson" at a window table for four. Ellen arranged herself with the stiffness of her

Charleston: The Dinner Table Trap

invalid persona, ordering tea and toast with her left hand. William stood at parade rest behind her chair, eyes scanning the room: a Prussian naval officer in braid, a rice planter with a gold-headed cane, a trio of merchants arguing cotton futures. Safe, for now.

At 7:30, the trap sprang.

The double doors swung open and in strode Enoch Grooms—six feet of brocade waistcoat and bourbon breath, the Macon slave trader who had sold William's brother in 1844 and bid $1,100 on Ellen at the 1846 auction. Grooms's eyes, small and piggish, swept the room like a hawk's. They locked on the "gentleman" with the sling.

"Well, bless my soul!" Grooms boomed, voice carrying to the chandeliers. "If it ain't young Johnson from Augusta! Your daddy's old friend, Enoch Grooms—don't you recall me from the Macon races last spring?"

Ellen's teacup froze halfway to her lips. The room tilted; the clatter of silverware became a roar in her ears. Grooms knew Dr. Collins intimately—shared brandy at the Eagle Tavern, swapped stories of "prime stock." One wrong word, one flicker of recognition, and the disguise would shatter. She coughed violently, buying three seconds of chaos. Tea sloshed onto the cloth; the Prussian officer glanced up, annoyed.

"Rheumatism's got my memory, sir," Ellen rasped, voice pitched low and gravelly, the drawl thickened with Charleston vowels. "And my voice. Fever's on me something fierce."

Grooms pulled out the chair opposite uninvited, his bulk eclipsing the sunlight. His two companions—factors from Savannah—hovered behind like crows. "Nonsense!" Grooms bellowed, slapping the table. "Sit, sit. Your man can fetch coffee." He snapped his fingers at William. "Boy, jump to it!"

William moved with mechanical obedience, but his eyes flicked to Ellen: *Stall.* He crossed to the sideboard, pouring coffee with exaggerated care, every second a prayer. Grooms leaned in, peering at the sling like a butcher inspecting livestock. "Heard your daddy sold that fancy girl of his—light-skinned wench, name of Ellen. Shame. She'd fetch two thousand in New Orleans, easy."

Ellen's pulse thundered. The sling—her genius, her salvation—hid the hand that had sewn her own freedom. She coughed again, a wet hack that sprayed droplets across the cloth. "Apologies," she croaked, dabbing with her left hand. "Fever's in my lungs. Doctor in Philadelphia's my only hope."

Grooms waved it off, undeterred. "No matter. Tell me, Johnson—why travel with just one nigger? Prime buck like yours ought to have a retinue. That boy—" he jabbed a thumb at William, returning with the pot—"he looks familiar. What's his name?"

Ellen seized the opening like a lifeline. "The rest took sick," she rasped, gesturing weakly at William. "Yellow fever swept the plantation. Left 'em in Augusta to die or recover. This one's all I trust with my medicine." She patted the sling, where a vial of laudanum—stolen from the mistress's cabinet—rattled convincingly.

William poured Grooms's coffee, hands steady despite the storm inside. Grooms squinted at him, then at the sling. Recognition flickered—William's height, the set of his shoulders—but the context was wrong. A white planter's valet, literate and calm? The pieces refused to fit. "Well," Grooms grunted, "mind the Charleston market. Prime bucks going for eighteen hundred. Your daddy ought to sell before prices drop."

The Prussian officer at the next table laughed, a sharp bark. "In Hamburg, we pay sailors, not own them!" The room tittered; Grooms flushed crimson, his pride pricked. Ellen seized the distraction. "My man'll settle the bill," she said, rising with theatrical weakness. "Business calls—estate papers in Wilmington."

She limped toward the door, cane tapping, William behind her. In the lobby, she collapsed onto a settee, spectacles askew, breath ragged. "He knew us," she whispered, voice breaking. "But he didn't," William answered, kneeling to adjust her sling. "The sling saved you. Whiteness saved us."

The first test of Charleston—the dinner table confrontation—was passed. A cough, a lie, and a slave trader's ego had bought them three hours. But the train to Wilmington waited, and the border loomed.

Charleston Hotel Lobby & Depot - 8:00 a.m. to 9:15 p.m., 22 December 1848

The Charleston Hotel lobby was a cathedral of marble and mahogany, its air thick with the scent of beeswax and cigar smoke. Ellen Craft—Mr. William Johnson—collapsed onto a velvet settee at 8:00 a.m., spectacles askew, the sling trembling against her chest. The encounter with Enoch Grooms had drained the last of her reserves; her cough was no longer acting but a raw scrape in her throat. William knelt beside her, ostensibly adjusting the mahogany case, but his hand brushed hers in a fleeting reassurance: *We're still here.*

Ellen removed the spectacles, wiping them with her left hand. Her eyes—red-rimmed, fierce—met William's. "He saw my face," she whispered. "If he thinks on it…" "He won't," William answered, voice low. "He saw a sick white man and a loyal slave. That's all the South lets him see." He glanced at the lobby clock: 8:05. The Wilmington train departed at 9:00 p.m.—thirteen hours to kill in a city crawling with traders.

They had planned for this. The Charleston Hotel parlor was neutral ground; white travelers came and went without question. Ellen ordered a private sitting room—$2, charged to "Mr. Johnson's" account—and retreated there with William as "valet." The room was small but safe: a sofa, a writing desk, a window overlooking Meeting Street. Ellen locked the door, then sank onto the sofa, the coat pooling around her like a verdict.

William set the case down and opened its false bottom. Inside: $6.50 in coins, the forged passes, the cedar scrap with their initials. He counted the money twice. "Enough for Wilmington tickets," he said. "Cabin for you, steerage for me. Twelve dollars total." Ellen nodded, removing the top hat. Her cropped hair clung damp to her scalp. "We board at eight-thirty. No more dining rooms."

The day passed in tense increments. Ellen napped fitfully, the sling her only pillow. William stood guard at the door, ears tuned to every footstep. At noon, a porter delivered a tray—biscuits, ham, coffee—paid with a dime from the stash. They ate in silence, the food ash in their mouths. At 3:00 p.m., Ellen practiced her cough in the mirror, perfecting the wheeze. William forged a new pass on hotel stationery: *Mr. W. Johnson, invalid, to Philadelphia via Wilmington. Servant William accompanying.* The ink dried slow in the humid air.

DISGUISED IN DAYLIGHT

At 6:00 p.m., they ventured out. Charleston's streets were alive with holiday bustle—carriages clattering, slaves hurrying with parcels, a brass band playing "Hark! The Herald Angels Sing" outside St. Michael's Church. Ellen kept the cane tapping, the cough rattling. William walked three paces behind, eyes scanning for Grooms's brocade waistcoat. None appeared.

At 7:30 p.m., they reached the Charleston & Wilmington depot—a cavern of brick and steam, lanterns swinging in the dusk. The ticket window was manned by a clerk named Mr. Silas Boone, a thin man with a ledger and a scowl. Ellen approached, leaning heavily on the cane. "Cabin to Wilmington," she rasped. "Myself and my man."

Boone slid the ledger forward. "Sign here. Pass for the boy."

Ellen coughed, extending the sling. "Rheumatism," she croaked. "Can't write. My man'll sign."

William produced the forged passes, hands steady. Boone squinted, then shrugged—white invalids were common this season. "Twelve dollars cabin, six steerage," he muttered. William counted out the coins—eighteen dollars total, the last of their hoard. Boone tore the tickets and waved them through.

At 8:45 p.m., the train pulled in—six cars, crimson paint, the *Wilmington Flyer*. Ellen boarded the first-class section, taking a window seat. William stowed the case in the colored car aft. The whistle shrieked at 9:00 sharp; the train lurched north, Charleston's lights receding into the dark.

In the cabin car, Ellen removed the spectacles, her reflection in the window a ghost. She touched the sling—her salvation, her shield. William, three cars back, carved a tiny notch into the case: *Charleston – survived*. The second test of the day—the lobby recovery and depot purchase—was passed. Eighteen dollars had bought them 140 miles of rail. But Wilmington waited, and with it, the border.

Wilmington Depot & Platform – 11:47 p.m., 22 December to 2:15 a.m., 23 December 1848

The *Wilmington Flyer* screeched into Wilmington, North Carolina, at 11:47 p.m., its brakes sparking against frost-slick rails. Steam hissed like a warning; the air carried pine smoke and the sharp bite of the Atlantic. Ellen Craft—Mr. William Johnson—pressed her face to the cabin car window, spectacles fogged,

Charleston: The Dinner Table Trap

the sling cradling an arm that ached from tension more than rheumatism. Charleston's dinner table trap lay 140 miles behind, but Wilmington was a slave port second only to Charleston—patrols thick, handbills fresh, every lantern a potential snare.

William, three cars back in the colored section, gripped the mahogany case and counted heartbeats. The schedule had slipped; the Richmond connection was delayed until 2:00 a.m. Two hours and thirteen minutes on a platform crawling with constables. The plan was to wait in the depot's colored waiting room, but a sign above the door read: NO COLORED AFTER 10 P.M. WITHOUT PASS. William's forged document would not withstand close scrutiny here.

Ellen descended first, cane tapping the platform, cough rattling like gravel in her throat. The depot swarmed: porters heaving trunks, a drunk slumped against a pillar, a deputy in a slouch hat pacing with a lantern. A handbill fluttered on the wall—VIGILANCE—ALL PASSES INSPECTED. RUNAWAYS IN DISGUISE. Ellen's pulse hammered. She limped toward the main waiting room, William trailing with the case.

Inside, a coal stove glowed. White passengers sprawled on benches; a clerk dozed behind the ticket window. Ellen took a seat near the stove, arranging herself like a man too ill for notice. William stood behind her, ostensibly guarding the luggage, eyes scanning. The deputy entered at 12:05, lantern swinging. "Passes!" he barked, voice cutting through snores.

White passengers grumbled, producing papers. Ellen extended her left hand, the forged doctor's certificate trembling slightly. The deputy—Mr. Elias Crowe, badge glinting—squinted at the sling, then at William's pass. "This your boy?" "My valet," Ellen rasped, coughing into the linen. "Loyal as they come. Taught him figures for the books."

Crowe's lantern hovered over William's face. "You look familiar, boy. What's your name?" "William, sir," he answered, head bowed. "Belong to Mr. Johnson of Augusta."

Crowe's eyes narrowed. He had patrolled Wilmington for ten years, knew every trader's stock. "Augusta, eh? Dr. Collins's man?" The name dropped like a stone. Ellen's blood turned to ice.

She coughed violently, doubling over, the sling shielding her face. "Fever's on me," she croaked, voice breaking. "Doctor in Philadelphia's my only hope. Delay'll kill me."

Crowe hesitated. White invalids were sacred; questioning one risked offense. The rice planter from Charleston, now awake, muttered, "Let the man be, Deputy. Some of us need sleep." Crowe grunted, moving on. Ellen exhaled silently. *Test one in Wilmington: passed.*

At 1:15 a.m., the depot emptied. Ellen and William retreated to the shadows near the stove. She removed the spectacles, wiping sweat from her brow. "He said Collins," she whispered. "But he didn't see us," William answered. "The sling, the cough—your armor held."

At 2:00 a.m., the Richmond train—a rattling string of wooden cars—pulled in. Ellen boarded the cabin section, taking a corner seat. William stowed the case in the colored car. The whistle blew at 2:15; the train lurched north, Wilmington's lanterns fading into the dark.

In the cabin car, Ellen touched the sling—her genius, her shield. William, aft, carved another notch into the case: *Wilmington – survived*. The third test of the journey—the platform inspection—was passed. The night stretched ahead, and Richmond waited.

Richmond to Philadelphia – 2:15 a.m., 23 December to Christmas Dawn, 25 December 1848

The Richmond-bound train clattered north through the Carolina night, its iron wheels singing a dirge over frost-hardened ties. Ellen Craft—Mr. William Johnson—sat in the first-class car, sling cradling her right arm, green spectacles reflecting the dim sway of oil lamps. The Wilmington deputy's question—*Dr. Collins's man?*—still echoed in her ears, a ghost that refused to die. Exhaustion pressed on her like a physical weight; her cough was raw, no longer entirely an act. Across the aisle, a Methodist minister muttered prayers; beside her, a Richmond merchant snored into his waistcoat.

William, three cars back in the colored section, clutched the mahogany case and counted mileposts in the dark. He had not slept since Macon; every jolt of the train was a reminder of the chains left behind. The cedar scrap with their initials lay hidden in the false bottom, the green thread at his wrist a silent vow. *Where you go, I go.*

At 6:00 a.m., December 23, the train jerked into Petersburg, Virginia. Snow flurried against the windows; passengers grumbled as they changed for the Richmond, Fredericksburg & Potomac line. Ellen descended, cane tapping, legs trembling beneath the coat. William followed, eyes scanning the platform. Richmond was the last slave state depot—patrols thick, the Potomac crossing a final gauntlet.

At 7:30 a.m., they boarded the Richmond train. Ellen took a window seat in the parlor car; William, the colored bench aft. The conductor, a stern man named Mr. Josiah Pike, checked tickets with a scowl. "Philadelphia?" he asked Ellen. "God willing," she rasped, coughing into the sling.

The train rolled north, crossing the James River into a landscape of bare fields and skeletal trees. At 10:00 a.m., it reached Aquia Creek, where a ferry waited to cross the Potomac. Virginia law mandated inspection of all colored passengers. Ellen's stomach knotted as they disembarked.

On the ferry, wind whipped the coat; the river's chop mirrored her nerves. A U.S. marshal, Mr. Caleb Reed, boarded with a clipboard. "Free papers or passes!" he demanded. William produced the forged documents, hands steady despite the storm inside. Reed's eyes narrowed. "This boy literate?" "Taught him figures for the plantation," Ellen croaked from the deck above, swaying on her cane. "Saves me trouble."

Reed hesitated, then waved them through. *Test one in Virginia: passed.*

At Aquia Creek, the final train—the Washington & Philadelphia—waited. Ellen boarded the parlor car, velvet seats and chandeliers a cruel mockery of her terror. William took the colored bench. The conductor, a kindly Quaker named Mr. Harlan, checked tickets again. "Philadelphia, sir?" "God willing," Ellen repeated, voice barely a whisper.

The train steamed north, crossing the Potomac into Maryland. Ellen felt the shift in the air—slave pens giving way to free soil. At 3:00 p.m., December 24, it crossed the Mason-Dixon Line. She felt it in her bones before Harlan announced it. She removed the spectacles, blinking at the light. William, sensing the change, smiled from the doorway.

The final crisis came at Havre de Grace, Pennsylvania border. A customs officer, Mr. Amos Grant, boarded at dusk, demanding signatures for baggage. Ellen coughed, extending the sling. "Rheumatism," she whispered. Grant, harried by holiday travelers, waved her through. William signed with a flourish: *W. Johnson. Test two: passed.*

At 4:17 a.m., Christmas Dawn, 1848, the train steamed into Philadelphia's Broad Street Station. Snow fell soft and silent, blanketing the city in white. Ellen descended, legs trembling, cane forgotten in the car. William followed, the mahogany case light as freedom.

They stood on the platform, two fugitives in broad daylight. Ellen looked at William, tears freezing on her lashes. "We're here," she said, voice breaking. "Where you go, I go," he answered, and for the first time, they embraced in public—husband and wife, free.

Abolitionist William Still waited with a carriage, alerted by a coded telegram from Charleston. "Welcome to liberty," he said, eyes wide at the disguise. Ellen laughed—a sound like church bells. William touched the cedar scrap in her pocket, the green thread at his wrist. The ledger was closed. The journey—1,000 miles, six tests, four days—was complete.

Philadelphia's snow kept falling, erasing their footprints. Behind them, Georgia's chains lay buried. Ahead, a new life, carved by love and courage, began.

Seven

The Overnight Train to Freedom

Wilmington Depot – *11:47 p.m., 22 December to 2:15 a.m., 23 December 1848*

The *Wilmington Flyer* screeched into Wilmington, North Carolina, at 11:47 p.m., its brakes sparking against frost-slick rails. A snowstorm—unseasonal, biblical—had swept down from the Appalachians, blanketing the coastal plain in white. Steam hissed from the locomotive like dragon's breath; the air carried pine smoke, coal dust, and the sharp bite of winter. Ellen Craft—Mr. William Johnson, Esquire—pressed her face to the cabin car window, green spectacles fogged, the sling cradling an arm that ached from tension more than rheumatism. Charleston's dinner table trap lay 140 miles behind, but Wilmington was a slave port second only to Charleston—patrols thick, handbills fresh, every lantern a potential snare.

William, three cars back in the colored section, gripped the mahogany case and counted heartbeats. The schedule had slipped; the Richmond connection was delayed until 2:00 a.m. due to snow on the tracks. Two hours and thirteen minutes on a platform crawling with constables. The plan was to wait in the depot's colored waiting room, but a sign above the door read: *NO COLORED AFTER 10 P.M. WITHOUT PASS.* William's forged document would not withstand close scrutiny here.

Ellen descended first, cane tapping the snow-dusted platform, cough rattling like gravel in her throat. The depot swarmed: porters heaving trunks, a drunk slumped against a pillar, a deputy in a slouch hat pacing with a lantern. A handbill fluttered on the wall—*VIGILANCE—ALL PASSES INSPECTED. RUNAWAYS IN DISGUISE.* Ellen's pulse hammered. She limped toward the main waiting room, William trailing with the case.

Inside, a coal stove glowed. White passengers sprawled on benches; a clerk dozed behind the ticket window. Ellen took a seat near the stove, arranging herself like a man too ill for notice. William stood behind her, ostensibly guarding the luggage, eyes scanning. The deputy—Mr. Elias Crowe, badge glinting—entered at 12:05, lantern swinging. "Passes!" he barked, voice cutting through snores.

White passengers grumbled, producing papers. Ellen extended her left hand, the forged doctor's certificate trembling slightly. Crowe squinted at the sling, then at William's pass. "This your boy?" "My valet," Ellen rasped, coughing into the linen. "Loyal as they come. Taught him figures for the books."

Crowe's lantern hovered over William's face. "You look familiar, boy. What's your name?" "William, sir," he answered, head bowed. "Belong to Mr. Johnson of Augusta."

Crowe's eyes narrowed. "Augusta, eh? Dr. Collins's man?" The name dropped like a stone. Ellen's blood turned to ice.

She coughed violently, doubling over, the sling shielding her face. "Fever's on me," she croaked, voice breaking. "Doctor in Philadelphia's my only hope. Delay'll kill me."

Crowe hesitated. White invalids were sacred; questioning one risked offense. A rice planter from Charleston, now awake, muttered, "Let the man be, Deputy. Some of us need sleep." Crowe grunted, moving on. Ellen exhaled silently. *Test one in Wilmington: passed.*

At 1:15 a.m., the depot emptied. Ellen and William retreated to the shadows near the stove. She removed the spectacles, wiping sweat from her brow. "He said Collins," she whispered. "But he didn't see us," William answered. "The sling, the cough—your armor held."

Outside, the snow thickened, swirling in eddies under the depot lamps. Railroad logs from the Library of Congress would later record: *Wilmington & Raleigh Railroad, 22 Dec 1848 – Train No. 4 delayed 2 hrs 15 min due to snow accumulation on tracks north of Rocky Point.* The delay was a curse and a blessing—more time exposed, but also more chaos to hide in.

At 2:00 a.m., the Richmond train—a rattling string of wooden cars—pulled in, its locomotive draped in icicles. Ellen boarded the cabin section, taking a corner seat. William stowed the case in the colored car. The whistle blew at 2:15; the train lurched north, Wilmington's lanterns fading into the white.

In the cabin car, Ellen touched the sling—her genius, her shield. William, aft, began to sing under his breath—a low, steady hymn he had learned in the Macon church gallery: *"Swing low, sweet chariot..."* The notes drifted through the cars, calming Ellen's frayed nerves. The first leg of the overnight journey—Wilmington to Richmond—was underway. But the border loomed.

Snowbound Tracks to Richmond – 2:15 a.m. to 6:00 a.m., 23 December 1848

The train clawed northward through a landscape erased by snow. Pines bent under white burdens; the tracks ahead vanished into a tunnel of swirling flakes. Inside the cabin car, the oil lamps guttered in the wind that leaked through warped window frames. Ellen Craft—Mr. William Johnson—sat rigid in her corner seat, the sling cradling her right arm, the green spectacles fogged with her own breath. The cough that had once been a performance now tore at her throat with real pain; the cold had settled deep in her lungs.

Across the aisle, the Methodist minister had fallen asleep again, his Bible open on his lap to Psalm 23. A Richmond merchant wrapped in a bearskin coat snored beside a crate of Carolina hams. Ellen's world narrowed to the rhythmic *clack-clack* of the wheels and the low, steady hum drifting from the colored car three doors back—William's voice, singing.

"Swing low, sweet chariot, comin' for to carry me home..."

The hymn floated through the darkness like a lifeline. Ellen closed her eyes, letting the melody anchor her. She pictured the pine clearing in Macon, the green thread knotted around their wrists, the cedar scrap with their initials. *Where you go, I go.* William's voice rose and fell with the train's sway, a cabinetmaker's precision in every note. He sang not for the other passengers—most were asleep—but for her, a secret serenade across iron and wood.

At 3:30 a.m., the train lurched to a halt. Snow had drifted across the tracks near Rocky Point; the conductor shouted for shovels. Ellen's heart seized. Delays meant exposure. She pressed her face to the frosted window. Lanterns bobbed in the storm; shadows of men swung picks against the rails. William's song paused, then resumed softer: *"A band of angels comin' after me..."*

Ellen wrapped the coat tighter, her teeth chattering. The cabin car grew colder; ice crystals formed on the inside of the glass. She whispered the words she dared not speak aloud: *If they search the cars... if they ask for signatures...* The sling was her shield, but it could not stop a thorough inspection.

At 4:15 a.m., the train inched forward again. The snow had eased to flurries, but the sky remained a leaden vault. Ellen dozed fitfully, dreaming of Macon's auction block, of Enoch Grooms's piggish eyes. She woke with a start at 5:00 a.m. as the train crossed the Roanoke River, the water black and swift beneath a lace of ice. Dawn was still hours away.

William's voice had grown hoarse, but he sang on: *"I looked over Jordan, and what did I see..."* The colored car was silent save for his hymn; the other passengers—field hands, cooks, a nursemaid—listened with closed eyes, drawing strength from the promise of a chariot that might carry them all.

At 5:45 a.m., the train slowed for Petersburg. Snow still fell, but the storm had spent its fury. Ellen adjusted the sling, rehearsing her bluff. The Richmond depot was next—Virginia soil, the last slave state. One more inspection, one more border, then the Potomac.

The train pulled into Petersburg at 6:00 a.m., its wheels crunching over packed snow. Ellen descended with the other cabin passengers, cane tapping the platform. William followed, the case heavy with exhaustion. The Richmond, Fredericksburg & Potomac line waited on an adjacent track, its locomotive already building steam. Ellen's legs trembled as she boarded the parlor car; William took the colored bench aft.

As the train lurched north, William's voice rose one final time: *"Comin' for to carry me home..."* The hymn faded into the hiss of steam and the crunch of snow. Ellen touched the sling, her talisman, and steeled herself for Richmond. The second leg of the overnight journey—snow-delayed, song-sustained—was complete. But the border guard waited.

Richmond Depot & Potomac Ferry – 7:30 a.m. to 11:00 a.m., 23 December 1848

The Richmond, Fredericksburg & Potomac train hissed into Richmond's Broad Street Station at 7:30 a.m., its locomotive draped in snow like a funeral shroud. The city lay hushed under a fresh six inches; church bells rang muffled across the James River. Ellen Craft—Mr. William Johnson—descended the parlor car steps with the stiffness of a man twice her age, cane tapping the icy platform, cough rattling in her chest. The sling cradled her right arm like a covenant; the green spectacles masked eyes that had not closed in thirty-six hours. Richmond was the last slave-state depot—patrols thick, the Potomac crossing a final gauntlet.

William followed three paces behind, the mahogany case balanced on his shoulder, his osnaburg shirt crusted with frost. His voice was raw from singing, but the hymn still echoed in his chest: *Comin' for to carry me home.* The colored car had emptied; field hands and cooks shuffled toward the slave pens for hire. William kept his eyes down, the forged pass burning a hole in his pocket.

The schedule allowed ninety minutes before the Aquia Creek ferry. Ellen limped toward the depot's main waiting room—a cavern of brick and coal smoke, its stove glowing like a forge. She took a bench near the fire, arranging herself like an invalid too weak for scrutiny. William stood behind her, ostensibly guarding the luggage, every muscle coiled.

At 8:00 a.m., a U.S. marshal—Mr. Caleb Reed, badge glinting beneath a wool greatcoat—boarded the platform with a clipboard. Virginia law mandated inspection of all colored passengers crossing the Potomac. "Free papers or passes!" he bellowed, voice cutting through the murmur of white travelers.

Ellen's heart seized. She extended her left hand, the forged doctor's certificate trembling. Reed squinted at the sling, then at William's pass. "This boy literate?" "Taught him figures for the plantation," Ellen croaked, coughing into the linen. "Saves me trouble."

Reed's lantern hovered over William's face. "Name?" "William, sir. Belong to Mr. Johnson of Augusta."

Reed's eyes narrowed. He had patrolled Richmond for fifteen years, knew Dr. Collins's stock. "Augusta, eh? Collins sold a cabinetmaker last year—tall buck, light hands. You him?"

William's pulse thundered, but his face remained stone. Ellen seized the moment, doubling over in a coughing fit that sprayed snow from her coat. "Fever's killing me," she rasped, voice breaking. "Doctor in Philadelphia's my only hope. Delay'll bury me."

Reed hesitated. White invalids were untouchable; questioning one risked scandal. A merchant in a beaver hat muttered, "Let the man board, Marshal. Some of us have business." Reed grunted, stamping the pass. *Test one in Richmond: passed.*

At 8:45 a.m., they boarded the ferry—a flatboat named *Potomac Queen*, its deck slick with ice. Ellen stood at the rail, wind whipping her coat, the river's chop mirroring her nerves. William, below with the luggage, touched the green thread at his wrist. *Where you go, I go.*

The ferry cast off at 9:15, cutting through gray water laced with ice floes. Richmond's spires receded; Maryland's shore loomed. Ellen's cough echoed over the water, a beacon and a shield. At 10:30 a.m., the *Queen* docked at Aquia Creek. The final train—the Washington & Philadelphia—waited on the Virginia side, its locomotive already building steam.

Ellen boarded the parlor car, velvet seats and chandeliers a cruel mockery of her terror. William took the colored bench aft. The conductor, a Quaker named Mr. Harlan, checked tickets. "Philadelphia, sir?" "God willing," Ellen rasped.

At 11:00 a.m., the train lurched north, snow still falling in soft, relentless curtains. Ellen touched the sling—her genius, her salvation. William, aft, began to hum under his breath: *"Swing low..."* The third leg of the overnight journey—Richmond depot, ferry crossing, border guard crisis—was complete. But the final border waited.

Washington to Philadelphia – 11:00 a.m., 23 December to Christmas Dawn, 25 December 1848

The Overnight Train to Freedom

The Washington & Philadelphia train steamed north from Aquia Creek at 11:00 a.m., its locomotive slicing through a landscape softened by snow. The Potomac's gray chop gave way to Maryland's fields, then Pennsylvania's farms—slave pens receding, free soil rising. Ellen Craft—Mr. William Johnson—sat in the parlor car, sling cradling her right arm, green spectacles reflecting the chandeliers' glow. The cough that had carried her 800 miles was now a rasp born of exhaustion and cold; her body trembled beneath the bottle-green coat. Yet every mile north loosened the chains around her heart.

William, three cars back in the colored section, clutched the mahogany case and felt the shift in the air. The hymn he had sung through the night—*Swing low, sweet chariot*—still hummed in his chest, softer now, a lullaby for the free man he was becoming. The cedar scrap with their initials lay hidden in the false bottom; the green thread at his wrist caught the lantern light. *Where you go, I go.*

At 1:00 p.m., the train crossed into Maryland. Ellen felt it before the conductor announced it—fewer overseers on the platforms, fewer handbills for runaways. She removed the spectacles, blinking at the light. A Quaker woman across the aisle smiled. "You'll be in Philadelphia by dawn, sir. Rest easy." Ellen nodded, the planter's drawl gone, her own voice a whisper: "God willing."

The train rolled through Baltimore at 3:00 p.m., snow still falling in soft curtains. Ellen dozed fitfully, dreaming of Macon's pine clearing, of William's hands carving their future. She woke at dusk as the train neared Havre de Grace, the Pennsylvania border. The final crisis loomed.

At 6:00 p.m., a customs officer—Mr. Amos Grant, harried by holiday travelers—boarded with a ledger. "Signatures for baggage!" he demanded. Ellen's stomach lurched. The sling was her shield, but a direct order to sign was a trap. She coughed violently, extending the linen. "Rheumatism," she rasped, voice barely audible. "Can't hold a pen."

Grant's eyes flicked to the sling, then to William, summoned from the colored car. "Your man'll sign," Ellen croaked. William stepped forward, producing the forged pass with a flourish. He signed the ledger: *W. Johnson, Esquire.* Grant, rushed and cold, waved them through. *Final test: passed.*

The train crossed the Susquehanna at 7:30 p.m., ice floes glinting under a rising moon. Ellen watched the river, tears freezing on her lashes. She touched the sling—her genius, her salvation—and whispered the vow: *Where you go, I go.* William, sensing her, hummed the hymn's final verse: *"Comin' for to carry me home..."*

At 10:00 p.m., the train passed Wilmington, Delaware—free soil, no inspections. Ellen removed the top hat, her cropped hair damp with sweat. She laughed, a sound like breaking chains. William, aft, carved a final notch into the case: *Freedom.*

The night stretched, snow softening the world outside. Ellen slept at last, the sling her pillow. William kept vigil, the mahogany case at his feet, the green thread his anchor.

At 4:17 a.m., Christmas Dawn, 1848, the train steamed into Philadelphia's Broad Street Station. Snow fell soft and silent, blanketing the city in white. Ellen descended, legs trembling, cane forgotten in the car. William followed, the case light as liberty.

They stood on the platform, two fugitives in broad daylight. Ellen looked at William, tears streaming. "We're here," she said, voice breaking. "Where you go, I go," he answered, and they embraced in public—husband and wife, free.

Abolitionist William Still waited with a carriage, alerted by a coded telegram from Charleston. "Welcome to liberty," he said, eyes wide at the disguise. Ellen laughed—a sound like church bells. William touched the cedar scrap in her pocket, the green thread at his wrist. The ledger was closed. The journey—1,000 miles, snowstorms, border guards, four days—was complete.

Railroad logs from the Library of Congress would later record: *Washington & Philadelphia Railroad, 24 Dec 1848 – Train No. 12 arrived Broad Street Station 4:17 a.m., on time despite snow delays.* But no log could capture the miracle of two souls who crossed a continent in disguise, sustained by love and a hymn.

Philadelphia's snow kept falling, erasing their footprints. Behind them, Georgia's chains lay buried. Ahead, a new life, carved by courage and cunning, began.

Eight

Philadelphia: First Breath of Freedom

Broad Street Station – 4:17 a.m. to 6:30 a.m., Christmas Dawn, 25 December 1848

The Washington & Philadelphia train exhaled its final hiss of steam at 4:17 a.m., Christmas Dawn, 1848, into the cavernous maw of Broad Street Station. Snow drifted through the open doors like manna, settling on the crimson cars and the frost-stiffened banners that read *PEACE ON EARTH*. Ellen Craft—still in the bottle-green coat, sling askew, top hat crushed in her left hand—stepped onto the platform as if descending from a dream. Her legs buckled; the cane clattered away. For the first time in twenty years, no overseer's bell, no auctioneer's gavel, no master's ledger governed her next breath.

William followed, the mahogany case light as liberty on his shoulder. His osnaburg shirt was rimed with ice, his eyes red from four nights without sleep, yet he stood tall—six feet of freed muscle and bone. The green thread at his wrist caught the station's gaslight, a wedding ring no law could sunder. He set the case down and reached for Ellen. She fell into his arms, spectacles fogging with tears that froze on her lashes.

"We are free," she whispered, the words foreign, sacred, impossible. "Where you go, I go," he answered, voice cracking like thin ice.

They embraced in public—husband and wife, no longer property. Passengers streamed past, some staring, most hurrying toward carriages and Christmas fires. A porter in a red cap paused, lantern raised. "You folks need help?" Ellen laughed—a sound like church bells after a storm. "We need everything," she said, "and nothing."

From the shadows near the ticket office stepped William Still—thirty-two, broad-shouldered, spectacles glinting, the Underground Railroad's meticulous archivist. He had received the coded telegram from Charleston two days prior: *Invalid gentleman & valet, arrive Christmas dawn.* Still's coat was dusted with snow; his breath plumed in the cold. He extended a gloved hand.

"Mr. and Mrs. Craft, I presume?" His voice was soft, deliberate, the tone of a man who had greeted hundreds of fugitives and knew the weight of first freedom. "William Still, Pennsylvania Anti-Slavery Society. Your chariot has arrived."

Ellen stared, uncomprehending. Snowflakes melted on her cropped hair—snow, a phenomenon she had only read about in stolen primers. She tilted her face to the sky, mouth open, catching flakes on her tongue like a child. "It's cold rain from heaven," she said, wonder breaking her voice.

Still smiled. "Welcome to Philadelphia. Come—there's a carriage."

He led them through the station's bustle—Quakers in broad brims, merchants in fur collars, a brass band tuning for a Christmas parade. Ellen walked without the cane, her limp forgotten. William carried the case, his free hand brushing hers with every step. Outside, a closed carriage waited, its driver a freedman named Isaac Hopper. Still helped Ellen inside, then William. The door shut; the world narrowed to velvet seats and the scent of coal smoke.

As the carriage rolled north on Broad Street, snow muffling the wheels, Still opened a ledger. "For the record," he said gently, "your names, ages, former owners, route taken. Every detail preserves your story—and aids those who follow."

Ellen removed the sling, flexing her right hand for the first time in public. "Ellen Craft, twenty-two. Born Eliza Smith's daughter, Colonel Ira Smith's property, Macon, Georgia." Her voice steadied with each word. "Disguised as

Philadelphia: First Breath of Freedom

Mr. William Johnson, invalid planter. Traveled by train, steamer, ferry—four days, 1,000 miles."

William added, "William Craft, twenty-four. Cabinetmaker, Dr. Robert Collins's property. Valet to Mr. Johnson." He touched the cedar scrap in his pocket. "We married in the woods, June 1846. No preacher, no paper—but God knew."

Still wrote in a neat, rapid hand, the quill scratching like a heartbeat. Snow tapped the carriage roof; church bells pealed across the city. At 5:30 a.m., they reached Still's home on North Fifth Street—a modest brick row house, its windows glowing with candlelight. His wife, Letitia, waited at the door with hot coffee and fresh cornbread.

Inside, the Crafts stood in the parlor, coats dripping, staring at a Christmas tree—fir branches adorned with paper stars and popcorn strings. Ellen touched a glass ornament, her reflection fractured in its curve. "It's beautiful," she whispered. "Like the world turned kind."

Letitia pressed mugs into their hands. "Drink. You're safe." William sipped, tears mixing with the coffee. "Safe," he repeated, the word a foreign country.

At 6:30 a.m., Still closed the ledger. "You'll stay here tonight—Christmas dinner with us. Tomorrow, we find work, a room, a new life." He paused. "The Fugitive Slave Law looms, but Philadelphia is a fortress. You are not alone."

Ellen looked at William, then at the snow beyond the window—falling still, erasing every trace of Georgia. She laughed again, the sound bright as breaking dawn. "We are free," she said, and this time, the words were a vow.

Still's Parlor & Christmas Breakfast – 6:30 a.m. to 10:00 a.m., 25 December 1848

The parlor of William Still's home on North Fifth Street glowed with the soft amber of whale-oil lamps and the flicker of a Yule log. Snow tapped the windowpanes like gentle fingers, sealing the world outside in white silence. Ellen Craft sat on a horsehair sofa, the bottle-green coat draped over the arm, her right hand—freed from the sling—flexing in wonder at its own motion. William stood behind her, one hand resting on her shoulder, the mahogany case at his feet like a relic from another life. The cedar scrap with their initials lay open on the tea table, the green thread untied and coiled beside it.

Letitia Still bustled in with a tray: cornbread still steaming, scrambled eggs flecked with chives, rashers of bacon, and a pot of coffee strong enough to wake the dead. "Eat," she commanded, her voice warm as the hearth. "Freedom's no good on an empty stomach."

Ellen stared at the food—more than she had seen at one table in her life. She lifted a fork with her right hand, the motion clumsy after days of concealment. The first bite of egg melted on her tongue; tears followed. William tore a piece of cornbread, butter dripping between his fingers. "Tastes like Sunday in the quarters," he said, voice thick, "only better."

Still sat opposite, ledger open, quill poised. "More details," he said gently. "Every station, every close call. The record must be exact." Ellen recounted the Macon depot, the forged passes, the purser's doubt in Savannah. William described the captain's scrutiny, the slave trader at breakfast, the border guard's lantern in Wilmington. Still wrote in a rapid, elegant hand, the quill scratching like a heartbeat. *Underground Railroad Records, Entry 1848-12-25: Crafts, William & Ellen, Macon GA to Philadelphia PA, disguised as invalid master & valet, 4 days, 1,000 miles, no capture.*

At 7:30 a.m., the Still children—four of them, ages three to ten—peeked around the doorframe, eyes wide at the strangers. Letitia shooed them back to their stockings, but the youngest, Caroline, toddled in with a rag doll. Ellen knelt, offering the child her freed hand. Caroline placed the doll in it. "Merry Christmas," the girl lisped. Ellen's laugh broke like sunrise.

William watched, a grin splitting his face. He lifted Caroline onto his knee, bouncing her gently. "First free Christmas," he said. "No bells, no whips, no ledger." Still closed the ledger. "Your choices now," he said. "Names, work, home. The Society will help."

Ellen touched the cedar scrap. "Names stay Craft," she said firmly. "Husband and wife, legal or not." William nodded. "Work—I'm a cabinetmaker. Hands still good." He flexed his scarred fingers. "Ellen sews, teaches, whatever frees others."

At 8:30 a.m., breakfast ended. Letitia cleared the plates; Still led them to a small bedroom under the eaves—two narrow beds, a washstand, a window overlooking a snow-laden apple tree. "Rest," he said. "Church at eleven, then Christmas dinner. Tomorrow, we find you a room on Lombard Street—colored boarding house, safe."

Ellen stood at the window, snowflakes drifting past like blessings. She had never seen snow fall; in Macon, winter was brown fields and chill winds. She pressed her palm to the cold glass, leaving a print that melted slowly. "It's a new world," she whispered. William joined her, arms around her waist. "Our world," he answered.

At 10:00 a.m., they lay on the beds—fully clothed, boots off, hands entwined across the gap. Sleep came like a tide, deep and dreamless. The green thread lay on the nightstand, the cedar scrap beneath Ellen's pillow. Outside, Philadelphia's church bells began to peal, calling the free to worship.

Still's records would later note: *Crafts slept 6 hours, first rest in liberty. Awakened smiling.*

Mother Bethel AME & Christmas Worship – 10:30 a.m. to 1:00 p.m., 25 December 1848

At 10:30 a.m., the Crafts descended the narrow stairs of William Still's home, transformed. Ellen wore a borrowed dress of dove-gray wool—Letitia's Sunday best, hemmed overnight—her cropped hair tucked beneath a simple bonnet. The sling was gone; her right hand, still pale from concealment, moved freely at her side. William had been given a clean white shirt and a charcoal waistcoat; his cabinetmaker's hands, scrubbed of sawdust, shone with soap. The mahogany case remained upstairs, but the cedar scrap and green thread rested in Ellen's pocket like talismans.

Still led them through snow-muffled streets to Mother Bethel African Methodist Episcopal Church on Sixth Street, the mother church of Black freedom, founded by Richard Allen in 1794. Carriages lined the curb; worshippers streamed in—freedmen in broadcloth, seamstresses in calico, children in mittens—their breath pluming in the cold. The steeple bell tolled eleven, its bronze voice rolling over the city like a benediction.

Inside, the sanctuary glowed with candlelight and pine boughs. Pews creaked under the weight of five hundred souls; the choir loft brimmed with voices rehearsing "Go Tell It on the Mountain." Ellen and William slipped into a back pew, Still beside them. Heads turned—new faces always drew notice—but smiles followed. A deacon pressed hymnals into their hands. Ellen opened hers with both hands, the right one trembling slightly. The pages smelled of ink and hope.

At 11:00 a.m., Reverend Daniel Alexander Payne ascended the pulpit, his robes black as midnight, his voice a trumpet. "On this Christmas morn," he intoned, "we celebrate not only the Babe in the manger, but every soul delivered from bondage!" The congregation roared *Amen!* Ellen's eyes filled; William's hand found hers, squeezing tight.

The choir launched into "Hark! The Herald Angels Sing," and Ellen's voice—soft, untrained, but true—joined the thousands. William's baritone, honed in Macon's colored gallery, rose beside her. For the first time, they sang in public as husband and wife, no fear of the lash for harmony.

During the sermon, Payne spoke of Moses and Pharaoh, of chains broken by divine hand. "Some of you," he said, eyes sweeping the pews, "crossed rivers of blood to sit here today. Some crossed in disguise, by train, by night. The Lord knows your names!" Ellen gripped William's hand; tears streaked her cheeks. Still leaned close. "He speaks of you," he whispered.

At noon, the offering plate passed. Ellen dropped in a silver dime—the last coin from their escape fund. William added a carved walnut button, whittled in the train's colored car. The deacon smiled, pocketing both.

Communion followed. Ellen and William approached the rail together, kneeling on the cushioned step. The bread was soft, the wine sweet. "The body of Christ, broken for you," the elder said. Ellen wept openly; William's shoulders shook. When they returned to the pew, a woman beside them—Mrs. Sarah Mapps Douglass, abolitionist and teacher—pressed a handkerchief into Ellen's hand. "Welcome home, sister," she murmured.

At 12:45 p.m., the service ended with "Joy to the World." The congregation spilled into the snowy street, voices echoing off brick facades. Children pelted snowballs; elders linked arms. Ellen and William stood on the church steps, faces tilted to the sky. Snowflakes melted on their lashes—Ellen's first, William's first in freedom.

Still guided them through the crowd. "You'll meet the Vigilance Committee tomorrow," he said. "Work, schooling, safety. But today—celebrate." A carriage waited to return them to North Fifth Street for Christmas dinner. As they climbed in, Ellen looked back at Mother Bethel's steeple, silhouetted against the white sky. "We worshipped as free people," she said, voice steady. William kissed her gloved hand. "And we'll worship tomorrow, and every day after."

The carriage rolled north, bells jingling from a passing sleigh. Philadelphia's snow kept falling, erasing every trace of Georgia. The third breath of freedom—public, sacred, shared—was complete.

Christmas Dinner & New Beginnings – 1:00 p.m. to 6:00 p.m., 25 December 1848

The Still household on North Fifth Street rang with the clamor of Christmas dinner at 1:00 p.m. The dining room—papered in faded rose, warmed by a crackling hearth—groaned under platters of roast goose, candied yams, collard greens, and cornbread stuffing. Letitia Still presided like a general, apron crisp, her four children darting between legs with wooden soldiers and peppermint sticks. Ellen and William Craft sat at the table's heart, no longer fugitives in disguise but honored guests, their places set with china and silver as if born to it.

Ellen wore the dove-gray dress, her right hand now steady as she passed the gravy boat. William, in the borrowed waistcoat, carved the goose with a cabinetmaker's precision—each slice even, elegant. The cedar scrap lay between their plates like a centerpiece; the green thread had been retied into a simple bracelet around Ellen's wrist. Snowlight filtered through lace curtains, gilding every face.

William Still raised a glass of cider. "To William and Ellen Craft," he toasted, voice resonant. "Who crossed a thousand miles of peril in four days, disguised by love and genius. May their freedom be the first of many." The children clinked mugs; Letitia's eyes shone. Ellen lifted her glass with both hands. "To the Underground Railroad," she said, "and to every soul still running." William added softly, "And to the pines in Macon that witnessed our vows."

They ate until plates were clean and belts loosened. The goose was succulent, the yams sweet as forgiveness. Ellen tasted cranberry sauce—

tart, bright, a flavor unknown in Georgia quarters—and laughed when it puckered her mouth. William fed her a bite of mince pie from his fork, their eyes locking in a promise older than the meal.

At 3:00 p.m., the table cleared, Still spread a city map across the cloth. "Your future," he said. "Lombard Street boarding house—$3 a month, colored, safe. William, the Vigilance Committee knows a furniture shop on Pine Street seeking a journeyman. Ellen, Mrs. Douglass teaches at the Institute for Colored Youth—sewing, reading, abolitionist work." He marked each spot with a quill dot.

Ellen traced the map with a freed finger. "School," she whispered. "I'll teach others to read the primers I stole." William nodded. "And I'll build tables that last—headboards carved with free names." He touched the cedar scrap. "Starting with ours."

Letitia brought coffee and plum pudding. The children performed a Nativity play—Caroline as the angel, her rag doll the Babe. Ellen clapped until her palms stung; William lifted the youngest onto his shoulders for the finale. Laughter filled the room, chasing the last shadows of bondage.

At 5:00 p.m., Still opened his ledger for the final entry. "Anything more?" he asked. Ellen leaned forward. "Write this: *On Christmas Day, 1848, Ellen and William Craft ate their first free meal, worshipped in their first free church, and planned their first free year. They owe their lives to courage, to each other, and to the Railroad that carried them home.*" William added, "And write: *They will never forget the cost of every mile.*"

Still wrote in his neat hand, then closed the book. *Underground Railroad Records, Entry 1848-12-25: Crafts, William & Ellen—arrived safe, housed, employed, enrolled in freedom. Story complete.*

At 6:00 p.m., dusk settled violet over the snow. The Stills walked the Crafts to their new room—a garret on Lombard Street, $3 paid in advance, a single window framing the city's spires. A narrow bed, a deal table, a stove already lit. Ellen stepped inside, turned in a slow circle, then laughed—a full, unfettered sound. William set the mahogany case down, opened it, and placed the cedar scrap on the table. "Our first furniture," he said.

They stood at the window, arms around each other, watching snow fall on a free city. Church bells pealed six; somewhere, a choir sang "Silent Night." Ellen rested her head on William's shoulder. "We are free," she said, the words no longer a question. "And we are home," he answered.

Philadelphia's snow kept falling, burying every trace of chains. The first full day of freedom ended not with a ledger's close, but with a door shut on the past and a window open to tomorrow.

Part Three

CELEBRITY & HUNTED

Nine

Boston: The Abolitionist Stage

Arrival & First Lecture – January 1849

The Boston & Worcester Railroad hissed into Boston's Kneeland Street Station on January 3, 1849, its cars dusted with the same snow that had greeted the Crafts in Philadelphia. Ellen and William Craft stepped onto the platform as celebrities in waiting—word of their escape, telegraphed by William Still, had preceded them like a comet. A delegation from the Boston Vigilance Committee waited: Theodore Parker, the transcendentalist minister with a prophet's beard; William Lloyd Garrison, editor of *The Liberator*, eyes blazing behind spectacles; and Wendell Phillips, orator and heir to a shipping fortune. Snow swirled around their top hats; the air rang with abolitionist fervor.

Garrison clasped William's hand. "Mr. Craft—your journey is the stuff of miracles." Ellen, in a new wool cloak and bonnet, smiled shyly. "We only walked through the door God opened." Parker laughed. "And slammed it on slavery's nose!"

They were whisked to the Marlboro Hotel—rooms paid by the Committee—then to Tremont Temple that evening. Two thousand souls packed the hall, gaslights blazing, banners reading *FREEDOM NOW*. Ellen's heart hammered; she had never addressed more than a dozen house servants. William squeezed her hand. "Speak from the pine clearing," he whispered. "They'll hear."

Garrison introduced them: "From the depths of Georgia bondage, disguised by genius and love—William and Ellen Craft!" The crowd roared. Ellen ascended the stage, legs trembling, her right hand—once hidden in a sling—now raised in greeting. She could not read the prepared remarks, but memory served.

"I stood on a Macon auction block," she began, voice soft but clear, "valued at twelve hundred dollars. My husband at fifteen hundred. We refused to be numbers." The hall fell silent; two thousand breaths held. She described the attic sewing, the forged passes, the slave trader inches away. "I wore whiteness like armor," she said, "but freedom was the weapon."

William followed, describing the cabinet shop loft, the midnight literacy lessons, the train whistle at 4 a.m. "Every mile," he said, "was carved by love." The crowd erupted; women wept; men pounded canes on the floor. *The Liberator* would report the next day: *"Never was a tale more thrilling, never a triumph more complete."*

Afterward, a daguerreotypist—Mr. Southworth & Hawes—set up in a side room. Ellen sat first, bonnet off, her light skin and cropped hair stark against black velvet. The plate captured her steady gaze—the eyes of a woman who had outwitted a nation. William stood beside her, hand on her shoulder, the cedar scrap visible in his pocket. The image would become abolition's icon: *The Fugitives Who Fooled the South.*

By January's end, they had spoken in Worcester, Salem, Lynn—crowds swelling to 2,000. Ellen's illiteracy was no barrier; her words, raw and rhythmic, moved hearts. William's baritone recounted details with a craftsman's precision. *The Liberator* printed excerpts weekly: *"Ellen Craft: 'I sewed my freedom stitch by stitch.'"*

Boston embraced them. They rented rooms on Southac Street, joined the Twelfth Baptist Church, and enrolled in a literacy class—Ellen's primer now her own. The stage was theirs, and the nation listened.

Daguerreotype Fame & Anti-Slavery Fairs – February 1849

The Southworth & Hawes daguerreotype—taken in Tremont Temple's side room on January 4—arrived polished and framed by February 1. Ellen sat

Boston: The Abolitionist Stage

in three-quarter profile, her light skin luminous against black velvet, eyes direct and unflinching; William stood behind her, hand on her shoulder, cedar scrap visible in his waistcoat pocket. The plate captured not just faces but defiance: *We escaped. We are here.* The image sold for twenty-five cents at every anti-slavery fair, pasted into albums, hung in parlors from Portland to Cincinnati. *The Liberator* ran it on the front page, February 9: *"Behold the Crafts—proof that genius and love outrun chains."*

Crowds swelled. By Valentine's Day, the Crafts spoke nightly—Faneuil Hall, Mechanics' Hall, even the State House steps when weather permitted. Two thousand souls packed each venue; latecomers stood in snow. Ellen's voice grew stronger, her illiteracy no hindrance. She spoke in cadences learned from Macon's colored gallery: *"I sewed my freedom stitch by stitch. I wore a white man's skin like Sunday best. But the heart underneath beat Black and free."* Women fainted; men wept; collection plates overflowed.

William's baritone grounded her. He described the cabinet shop loft, the forged passes, the train whistle at 4 a.m. "Every mile," he said, "was measured in love and risk." Together, they were abolition's living sermon.

Anti-slavery fairs became their stage. The Boston Female Anti-Slavery Society's annual bazaar at Faneuil Hall, February 14–16, raised $2,000. Ellen sat at a table piled with pincushions, needlebooks, and abolitionist samplers—each stitched by her own hand. *"Buy freedom one stitch at a time,"* she told buyers. William demonstrated a walnut lap desk with a secret compartment—*"For hiding primers, or passes."* Children pressed coins into their palms; matrons wept over the daguerreotype.

Garrison printed their speeches weekly. *The Liberator,* February 23: *"Ellen Craft, though unable to read, speaks with the eloquence of truth. William Craft, cabinetmaker, builds arguments as finely jointed as his furniture."* Invitations poured in—New Bedford, Providence, New York. The Crafts traveled by rail, always together, always watched by friendly eyes.

In their Southac Street rooms, Ellen practiced letters by lamplight—*W, E, C*—her primer now her own. William carved a headboard for their bed: *W.C. & E.C., 1849, Free.* The daguerreotype hung above the mantel, a mirror of their new selves.

Boston crowned them. The stage was theirs, and the nation listened.

Spring Speaking Tour & Literacy Gains – March–April 1849

March roared in like a lion, but the Crafts rode its winds. By the ides, they were on the lecture circuit—Providence, Hartford, Springfield—each hall packed to the rafters with 2,000 souls hungry for their story. The Boston & Providence Railroad became their chariot; Garrison's introductions their herald. In Hartford, Ellen spoke beneath a banner stitched by local women: *GENIUS IN A BONNET*. She no longer needed notes; memory and passion sufficed. "I stood on a Georgia block," she told the crowd, "priced like cattle. But love is priceless, and it carried us north." Applause shook the rafters; collection plates brimmed.

William's role deepened. He demonstrated the mahogany traveling case—false bottom revealed to gasps—then passed it through the audience. "Hide your primers here," he said, "or your passes, or your hope." In Springfield, a cabinetmaker offered him a shop apprenticeship; William declined with grace. "My hands build freedom now," he said, "one speech at a time."

Literacy lessons intensified. Back in Boston, Ellen attended Mrs. Sarah Mapps Douglass's evening class at the Institute for Colored Youth. Three nights a week, she traced letters by gaslight: *cat, mat, freedom*. Her primer—once stolen from the Big House attic—now bore her own handwriting in the margins: *The Crafts are free*. By April, she could sign her name in a clear, looping script. William, already fluent, taught her fractions using lumber measurements: *"Three boards, 7/8 inch thick—how many feet?"* She solved it aloud, triumphant.

Garrison mentored them privately. Sunday suppers at his Roxbury home became strategy sessions. Over roast lamb, he coached Ellen's cadence: "Pause after 'auction block'—let them feel the hammer." To William: "Describe the train whistle—make them hear it." *The Liberator* printed their progress: *March 16:* "Ellen Craft now reads simple sentences; her voice grows bolder." *April 6:* "William Craft's oratory rivals Phillips."

Spring fairs multiplied. The New England Anti-Slavery Convention in May billed them as headliners. Ellen stitched a sampler for the auction block: *WHERE YOU GO, I GO—RUTH 1:16*. It fetched $50. William carved a miniature railroad car with a hidden compartment; it sold for $30. Their fame spread; daguerreotypes sold out in New York.

In their Southac Street rooms, Ellen practiced speeches before a mirror, bonnet off, hair growing into soft curls. William planed a walnut cradle—*for the children we'll have in freedom*. The headboard above their bed now read: W.C. *&* E.C., 1849, Free *&* Learning.

Boston's abolitionist stage was theirs, and spring carried their voices farther than any train.

May Convention Climax *&* Book Deal – May 1849

The New England Anti-Slavery Convention opened May 29, 1849, in Faneuil Hall, the cradle of liberty itself. Gaslights blazed; banners of crimson and gold draped the rafters; 2,500 abolitionists filled every inch—standing room only, windows cracked despite the spring chill. William Lloyd Garrison presided like a conductor; Wendell Phillips, Theodore Parker, and Frederick Douglass flanked the platform. But the evening belonged to the Crafts.

At 8:00 p.m., Garrison raised his hand. "From the pine woods of Georgia to the freedom of Boston—William and Ellen Craft!" The hall erupted. Ellen ascended in a new dress of deep blue silk—stitched by her own hand, no sling, no disguise. Her hair had grown into soft ringlets; her eyes shone with the confidence of a woman who had read her first full sentence aloud the night before. William followed in a tailored black coat, cedar scrap pinned inside the lapel like a medal.

Ellen spoke first. "I cannot read the words on your banners," she began, voice ringing clear, "but I can read the hope in your faces." She recounted the attic sewing, the forged passes, the slave trader inches away. "I wore a white man's skin," she said, "but the soul beneath was always mine." The crowd roared; Douglass leapt to his feet, clapping until his palms bled.

William followed with the cabinet shop loft, the midnight literacy, the train whistle at 4 a.m. He opened the mahogany case on stage—false bottom revealed to gasps—then passed it through the front row. "This carried our freedom," he said. "Now it carries your donations." Coins rained into the compartment.

The climax came at 10:00 p.m. Garrison announced a book deal: *Running a Thousand Miles for Freedom*, to be written by the Crafts with Garrison's editorial hand. "Their story in their words," he declared. "Proceeds to the cause." Cheers shook the hall; the daguerreotype was projected on a screen—Ellen's gaze, William's hand on her shoulder—drawing tears and pledges.

Personal milestones crowned the month. On May 15, Ellen read her first full page aloud—Garrison's *Liberator* editorial about their escape. On May 20, William completed the walnut cradle, carving *W.C. & E.C., Free 1849* on the headboard. On May 25, they signed the book contract—Ellen's looping signature beside William's steady hand.

The Liberator, June 1: *"The Crafts' convention triumph—2,500 souls moved, $1,200 raised, book to follow. Ellen reads; William builds; freedom grows."*

Boston's stage had launched them; the nation awaited their book.

Book Writing, Summer Tour & Lasting Legacy – June–December 1849

June 1849 dawned humid and bright, and the Crafts' book took shape in Garrison's Roxbury study. Mornings, Ellen dictated while William transcribed—her words raw, rhythmic, unlettered but electric. "I sewed the coat in the attic," she said, "each stitch a prayer." William added measurements: *"Mahogany case, 18 x 12 x 9 inches, false bottom 1/4 inch clearance."* Afternoons, Garrison edited, sharpening prose without dulling truth. By July 4, the manuscript—*Running a Thousand Miles for Freedom*—was half done, 200 pages of escape and love.

The summer tour began July 10: Portland, Bangor, Albany—2,000-person crowds in every hall. Ellen now read excerpts aloud, her voice steady, primer conquered. In Portland, she signed fifty copies with her looping *Ellen Craft*; William carved a miniature cedar scrap for each buyer. *The Liberator*, August 17: *"Ellen reads her own words; the hall weeps."*

In Albany, a publisher offered $5,000 advance—rejected. "Proceeds to the cause," William said. Instead, they donated $1,000 to the Vigilance Committee. Ellen stitched a quilt for auction: *1,000 MILES, 1,000 STITCHES*. It fetched $300.

Personal milestones crowned the season. On August 1, Ellen read the entire Book of Ruth aloud—*"Where you go, I go"*—tears streaming. On September 15, William opened a small cabinet shop on Cambridge Street, hiring two fugitive apprentices. On October 1, the book went to press—10,000 copies, frontispiece the famous daguerreotype.

By December, *Running a Thousand Miles* sold out its first printing. Reviews poured in: *New York Tribune*: "A thriller penned by its heroes." British abolitionists ordered 5,000 copies. The Crafts spoke at Faneuil Hall again—2,500 souls, standing ovation lasting seven minutes. Ellen closed: "We ran for ourselves, but we speak for millions still in chains."

Their legacy hardened. The daguerreotype hung in parlors nationwide; Ellen's sampler adorned Garrison's office; William's cradle—now with a newborn's name, *Hope Craft, born November 1849*—stood in their Southac Street nursery. *The Liberator*, December 28: *"1849: The Year of the Crafts. Their story, their child, their freedom—abolition's living proof."*

Boston's stage had launched them; the world now carried their voice. The pines of Macon were a memory, but the cedar scrap on their mantel—*W.C. & E.C., Free 1849*—whispered eternity.

Ten

The Fugitive Slave Act

Washington & Boston – September 1850

The Compromise of 1850 passed the U.S. Senate on September 18, 1850, its Fugitive Slave Act a venomous clause buried in legislative compromise. The *Congressional Globe* recorded Daniel Webster's oratory: *"This law will be executed in all its parts... restoring to the South what is justly theirs."* In Boston, the news hit like a thunderclap on September 20. William Craft read the broadside aloud in their Southac Street parlor, voice steady but knuckles white on the page: *"Any person aiding a fugitive—$1,000 fine, six months imprisonment. Federal marshals empowered. Free states now complicit."*

Ellen, cradling nine-month-old Hope in her lap, felt the room tilt. The baby gurgled, unaware that freedom's cradle had just been kicked. "They'll come for us," she whispered. William touched the framed cedar scrap on the mantel—*W.C. & E.C., Free 1849.* "Let them try. Boston is not Macon."

Two weeks later, October 3, slave catchers Willis Hughes and John Knight—deputized by Georgia—stepped off the New York steamer at Long Wharf. Hughes was a Macon deputy, thick-necked, eyes like wet slate, warrant in his coat pocket: *William Craft, 26, cabinetmaker, property of Dr. Robert Collins.* Knight, a Charleston trader, lean and mean, carried Ellen's: *Ellen Craft, 24, seamstress, property of Mrs. Ira Smith.* Both warrants bore a Massachusetts judge's seal, compelled by the Act.

The hunters moved fast. They bribed a hack driver for the Crafts' address, staked out Tremont Temple, shadowed Twelfth Baptist Church. Garrison received word first—telegraphed from Philadelphia by William Still—and called an emergency Vigilance Committee meeting, October 10, at Theodore Parker's West Roxbury church. Two hundred abolitionists gathered, armed with resolutions and revolvers.

Ellen stood before them, Hope on her hip, bonnet in hand. "We ran once," she said, voice clear despite fear. "We'll fight now." William added, "Boston is our pine clearing. We stand."

The Committee acted. Lewis Hayden, a fugitive turned firebrand, hid the Crafts in his Beacon Hill home—false wall behind the parlor stove. Parker preached a sermon titled *"The Law of God vs. the Law of Devils,"* quoting Scripture and brandishing a pistol. Hughes and Knight were mobbed on Court Street—tar rumored, feathers promised. By October 25, they fled to New York, warrants unfilled.

But the Act's shadow lingered. Ellen sewed by candlelight, every stitch defiance. William planed wood in Hayden's cellar, each joint a promise. The hunters were gone—for now.

Hunters' Return & Boston Resistance – October 26–November 10, 1850

The hunters did not stay gone.

On October 26, Willis Hughes and John Knight returned to Boston, reinforced. A federal marshal, Mr. Patrick Riley—Irish, broad as a barrel, badge gleaming—accompanied them, armed with new warrants and a posse of six deputies. The *Congressional Globe* had emboldened them: *"Commissioners appointed... $10 for every fugitive returned."* Hughes licked his lips at the bounty—$300 each for the Crafts, alive.

They struck at dawn, October 28. Riley's posse raided the Southac Street rooms—door splintered, cradle overturned, Ellen's primer torn. The family was already gone, spirited to Lewis Hayden's Beacon Hill cellar the night prior. Hayden, pistol in hand, met the marshals with a grin. "Come closer," he said, "and meet Mr. Colt." The posse retreated, cursing.

Boston erupted. Garrison's *Liberator*, November 1: *"HUNTERS IN OUR MIDST—CITIZENS, ARM!"* Handbills plastered every corner: *WILLIAM & ELLEN CRAFT—KIDNAPPED IN SPIRIT*. Two thousand rallied at Faneuil Hall, November 3. Theodore Parker thundered: "This Act makes every Northerner a slave-catcher!" Wendell Phillips proposed a resolution: *"We will not obey."* It passed unanimously.

Ellen, hidden in Hayden's attic with Hope, sewed a new disguise—Quaker gray, bonnet deep. William forged letters in the cellar: *"Mr. Johnson, invalid, bound for England."* The Vigilance Committee smuggled food, funds, false papers. On November 5, Hughes cornered William Lloyd Garrison on State Street—grabbed his coat, demanded the Crafts' location. A crowd of dockworkers intervened; Hughes fled with a bloody nose.

By November 7, the city was a tinderbox. Riley posted $1,000 reward broadsides: *WILLIAM CRAFT—6 ft, scar on wrist. ELLEN CRAFT—light skin, speaks well.* Churches rang alarm bells; Black militias drilled in secret. Ellen, sleepless, rocked Hope by candlelight. "We cannot stay," she whispered to William. He nodded, carving a final notch into the mahogany case: *Boston – besieged.*

November 10, the Committee decided: exile. Passages booked on the *Cambria*, Cunard Line, sailing November 15 for Liverpool. Lewis Hayden pressed $50 into William's hand. "England's soil is free," he said. "Go."

The hunters prowled, but Boston's resistance held. The second act of the crisis—raids, rallies, resolve—was complete. Flight loomed.

Escape to the Docks & Stormy Atlantic – November 11–December 2, 1850

The plan crystallized at midnight, November 11, in Lewis Hayden's Beacon Hill cellar. The Vigilance Committee mapped every step: false names, disguised routes, armed escorts. Ellen would travel as "Miss Eliza Johnson," a Quaker invalid; William as her "manservant, James Brown." Hope, bundled in blankets, would be "the child of a committee member." The mahogany case—now lined with abolitionist pamphlets—held their few possessions: the cedar scrap, Ellen's primer, William's carving tools.

At 3:00 a.m., November 13, a closed carriage rolled to Hayden's back door. Theodore Parker, pistol tucked in his coat, climbed in first. "Godspeed," he whispered, pressing a Bible into Ellen's hands—inside, $20 and a note: *"Where you go, I go."* The driver, a freedman named Robert Morris, cracked the reins. Snow had turned to sleet; Boston's streets gleamed black.

They reached Long Wharf at 4:30 a.m. The *Cambria* loomed, Cunard's pride, 1,400 tons, paddlewheels still. Captain Charles Judkins—tipped by Garrison—waited at the gangplank. "Cabins 12 and 14," he muttered, waving them aboard without papers. Riley's posse patrolled the wharf, lanterns swinging, but Morris's carriage bore Vigilance Committee colors; the deputies hesitated. Parker's pistol glinted. The hunters backed off.

Aboard, Ellen collapsed in Cabin 12, Hope fussing against her breast. William stowed the case in Cabin 14, then stood guard at the door. At 6:00 a.m., the *Cambria* cast off, Boston Light receding into gray. Ellen watched from the porthole, tears mixing with sleet. "We ran again," she whispered. William touched the cedar scrap. "This time, to stay free."

The Atlantic greeted them with fury. November 15, a gale struck—waves forty feet, the ship pitching like a drunk. Passengers retched; crockery shattered. Ellen, seasick but defiant, sang to Hope: *"Swing low..."* William lashed the case to the bunk, carving notches for each storm day. On November 20, the mainmast cracked; sailors prayed. Ellen clutched Parker's Bible, reading aloud—her voice the only steady thing.

By November 28, the storm broke. Sun pierced the clouds; porpoises raced the bow. Ellen stood on deck, wind whipping her bonnet, Hope asleep in a sling. William joined her, arm around her waist. "England," he said, pointing to gulls wheeling ahead.

December 2, the *Cambria* steamed into Liverpool, docks bristling with masts. British abolitionists—led by John Estlin—waited with banners: WELCOME, CRAFTS! No warrants, no chains. Ellen stepped onto free soil, knees buckling. William caught her. "We are here," he said. "Where you go, I go," she answered, and they walked into England's embrace.

The third act—escape, storm, safe harbor—was complete. A new chapter waited.

Liverpool Welcome & New Life in England – December 2, 1850–1851

The *Cambria* docked at Liverpool's Prince's Pier on December 2, 1850, under a pale winter sun. British abolitionists—John Estlin, a Bristol merchant with a Quaker's calm; Mary Estlin, his daughter, eyes bright with purpose—waited on the quay. Banners fluttered: WELCOME, WILLIAM & ELLEN CRAFT—HEROES OF FREEDOM. No marshals, no warrants, only open arms and steaming tea. Ellen stepped onto English soil—solid, free—her knees buckling with the weight of arrival. Hope, now ten months, cooed in her sling. William steadied Ellen, the mahogany case light in his grip. "We are here," he said, voice breaking. "Where you go, I go," she answered, and they walked into England's embrace.

The Estlins whisked them to a Clifton boarding house—rooms with coal fires, a cradle for Hope, a desk for William's tools. That night, a welcome supper: roast beef, Yorkshire pudding, and speeches. Estlin toasted: "You crossed an ocean of storms; Britain is your harbor." Ellen, in a new wool dress, spoke briefly: "We ran from chains, but love carried us." The room cheered; a reporter from *The Bristol Mercury* scribbled every word.

By December 10, the Crafts were celebrities again. Invitations flooded—Bristol, London, Manchester. Ellen's illiteracy was no barrier; her voice, honed in Boston halls, moved thousands. William demonstrated the mahogany case at every lecture, false bottom revealed to gasps. *The Times*, December 20: *"The Crafts' tale—1,000 miles, one storm, one love—stirs Britain's soul."*

A new life took root. In January 1851, they settled in Ockham, Surrey, under the wing of the British and Foreign Anti-Slavery Society. William opened a furniture shop—*Craft & Son, Est. 1851*—carving headboards with *Free 1848*. Ellen enrolled in a ladies' school, mastering reading and writing in six months. By spring, she penned letters to Garrison: *"I sign my name with pride—Ellen Craft."*

Hope thrived, toddling through daffodils. Two more children followed—Charles in 1852, Brougham in 1854. Ellen taught sewing to fugitive women; William trained apprentices, Black and white. Their book, *Running a Thousand Miles for Freedom*, sold 30,000 copies in Britain, funding schools in Jamaica. The cedar scrap hung above their mantel, now engraved: *W.C. & E.C., Free Forever.*

The Fugitive Slave Act

The Fugitive Slave Act could not touch them. Hughes and Knight were forgotten; Boston's siege a memory. In 1860, the Crafts published a second edition, dedicated to John Brown. In 1868, they returned to the U.S., buying a Georgia plantation to teach freedmen—full circle, chains broken.

Liverpool's welcome had planted them; England's soil grew them. The final act—exile, rebirth, legacy—was complete. The pines of Macon were a lifetime away, but the green thread around Ellen's wrist whispered eternity.

Eleven

Boston: The Siege

The Hunters Arrive & Armed Vigil – October 3–15, 1850

The Fugitive Slave Act became law on September 18, 1850, but its teeth sank into Boston on October 3. At dawn, Willis Hughes and John Knight—Georgia's bloodhounds, now federal deputies—stepped off the New York steamer at Long Wharf, warrants clenched like claws. Hughes, thick-necked and pig-eyed, carried William's: *Property of Dr. Robert Collins, $1,500 reward.* Knight, lean as a whip, bore Ellen's: *Property of Mrs. Ira Smith, $800.* A U.S. marshal, Patrick Riley, badge gleaming, led the posse of six. The *Congressional Globe* had armed them; Boston would bleed.

William Craft read the news in Garrison's *Liberator* at 7:00 a.m., Southac Street parlor. Ellen, nursing nine-month-old Hope, felt the walls close. "They're here," she whispered. William touched the cedar scrap on the mantel. "Then we fight."

The Vigilance Committee mobilized by noon. Theodore Parker—transcendentalist minister, six feet of righteous fury—convened two hundred at his West Roxbury church. "The Act makes every citizen a slave-catcher," he thundered, pistol on the pulpit. "We answer with resolve—and if need be, lead." Lewis Hayden, fugitive turned firebrand, volunteered his Beacon Hill home as fortress. Armed guards—Black and white, dockworkers and divines—took shifts at the Crafts' door.

October 5, Hughes raided Twelfth Baptist Church during Sunday service. William, preaching from the gallery, spotted him. "There's the devil!" he shouted. Congregants surged; Hughes fled, coat torn. Parker's letter to the Massachusetts Historical Society, October 6: *"Hughes met Boston's wrath—barely escaped with his skin."*

By October 10, the Crafts' home was a citadel. Barricades of furniture blocked windows; muskets leaned in corners. Ellen sewed by candlelight, stitching Quaker gray for disguise. William carved notches into the mahogany case: *Siege Day 1, Day 2...* Guards rotated—Hayden with a Bowie knife, Parker with his Colt revolver. Hope slept in a cradle lined with *The Liberator*.

October 12, Riley's posse stormed Southac Street at midnight. Doors splintered; lanterns swung. Hayden met them on the stairs, dynamite fuse in hand—bluff or bomb, no one dared test. "One step," he roared, "and we all meet God!" The posse retreated, cursing. Parker's letter, October 13: *"Hayden's fuse saved the night—Boston stands."*

October 15, the siege tightened. Hughes bribed a hack driver; Knight shadowed Garrison. The Committee decided: the Crafts must vanish. A coffin was ordered—oak, brass handles, secret air holes. The first act—hunters' arrival, armed vigil—was complete. Escape loomed.

The Coffin Plan & Final Raid – October 16–20, 1850

The coffin arrived at Lewis Hayden's Beacon Hill home on October 16, 1850—oak, six feet long, brass handles polished to a funeral gleam. Inside, a false bottom concealed air holes and a thin mattress; a hidden latch allowed escape from within. The undertaker, Mr. Jonas Fletcher—a Vigilance Committee ally—delivered it with a wink. "For Mr. Johnson's 'ailing aunt,'" he said. Ellen touched the wood, steadying her breath. "I've worn death before," she whispered, recalling the sling. "This time, it carries me to life."

The plan was audacious: Ellen and Hope in the coffin, William as "mourner" in Quaker gray, escorted by armed abolitionists to Long Wharf. The *Cambria*, Cunard Line, sailed November 15; passage was booked under false names. Theodore Parker's letter to Charles Sumner, October 17 (Massachusetts Historical Society): *"A coffin for the living—poetic justice against the Act that buries freedom."*

October 17, Hughes struck again. At dusk, Riley's posse—now eight strong—raided the Crafts' Southac Street rooms. Furniture overturned, cradle smashed, Ellen's primer shredded. The family was already gone, smuggled to Hayden's cellar at dawn. Parker's guards repelled the intruders with musket butts; Knight took a blow to the jaw. *The Liberator*, October 18: "HUNTERS FOILED—SOUTHAC STREET STANDS."

October 18, the coffin was tested. Ellen lay inside with Hope, latch practiced, air holes checked. Thirty minutes—claustrophobic, heart-pounding—but survivable. William paced, carving *Siege Day 13* into the mahogany case. Guards drilled in the alley: Hayden, Parker, Robert Morris—pistols, rifles, resolve.

October 19, the final raid. At 11:00 p.m., Hughes scaled Hayden's back fence, Riley at the front door with a warrant. Parker met them on the stoop, Colt revolver cocked. "One step," he roared, "and I send you to your Maker!" Hayden ignited a dynamite fuse—real this time—sparks hissing. The posse froze; neighbors poured into the street, armed with pokers and prayers. Hughes fled, coat aflame from a thrown lantern. Parker's letter, October 20: "The hunters ran like rabbits—Boston's fire lit their heels."

Midnight, October 20. The coffin was loaded into a hearse—black curtains, muffled wheels. Ellen and Hope inside, latch ready. William, in Quaker gray, rode shotgun beside Morris. Parker and six guards formed the cortege, muskets hidden under coats. The procession rolled through silent streets, snow beginning to fall. At Long Wharf, Captain Judkins waited, *Cambria*'s gangplank down. The coffin was carried aboard as "cargo for Liverpool"—no questions, $50 bribe.

Ellen emerged in Cabin 12, Hope fussing, air sweet with salt. William stowed the case in Cabin 14. At 2:00 a.m., the *Cambria* cast off, Boston Light fading into the dark. Ellen watched from the porthole, tears freezing on her cheeks. "We buried Georgia tonight," she said. William touched the cedar scrap. "And rose in England."

The second act—coffin plan, final raid, midnight flight—was complete. The Atlantic waited.

Stormy Crossing & Liverpool Arrival – October 20–December 2, 1850

The *Cambria* slipped from Long Wharf at 2:00 a.m., October 20, 1850, her paddlewheels churning black water into froth. Boston's lights dwindled to pinpricks, then vanished. Ellen Craft emerged from the coffin in Cabin 12, Hope clutched to her breast, lungs gulping free air. The oak box—brass handles cold, false bottom scarred—stood in the corner like a silent sentinel. William, still in Quaker gray, latched the door and carved *Siege Ended* into the mahogany case. Snow hissed against the porthole; the Atlantic welcomed them with a roar.

Captain Charles Judkins, tipped by Garrison, kept the Crafts' secret. "Cabins 12 and 14—paid in full," he muttered, waving off curious stewards. Ellen collapsed on the bunk, Hope nursing, the baby's warmth the only steady thing. William stood guard, cedar scrap in his pocket, pistol borrowed from Parker tucked in his waistband. The ship pitched; lanterns swung. "We're coffin-born again," Ellen whispered. William kissed her forehead. "And ocean-bound to life."

The Atlantic answered with vengeance. October 22, a nor'easter struck—winds seventy knots, waves forty feet, the *Cambria* groaning like a dying beast. Passengers retched in corridors; crockery shattered. Ellen, seasick but defiant, sang to Hope: *"Swing low, sweet chariot..."* The coffin, lashed to the bulkhead, rattled with every roll. William braced the case, carving notches for storm days: *Day 1, Day 2...* On October 25, the main topmast cracked; sailors clung to rigging, praying in three languages. Ellen clutched Parker's Bible—*"Where you go, I go"*—reading aloud by candle stub, her voice the ship's only calm.

November 1, the storm broke. Sun pierced the clouds; porpoises raced the bow. Ellen stood on deck, wind whipping her bonnet, Hope asleep in a sling of Quaker gray. William joined her, arm around her waist. "England," he said, pointing to gulls wheeling ahead. The crew cheered; Judkins raised a toast with rum. Theodore Parker's letter to the Massachusetts Historical Society, November 15: *"The Crafts sail through hell's own gale—freedom their north star."*

November 10, the Irish coast rose—green cliffs, white foam. Ellen read the primer aloud, her voice steady: *"The ship sails to free land."* William carved a final notch: *Storm Survived.* Hope toddled on the deck, first steps on a free ship.

December 2, the *Cambria* steamed into Liverpool's Prince's Pier under a pale winter sun. British abolitionists—John Estlin, Mary Estlin—waited with banners: WELCOME, HEROES OF FREEDOM. No warrants, no chains. Ellen stepped onto English soil, knees buckling. William caught her, the coffin carried ashore as "cargo." Reporters swarmed; *The Bristol Mercury* scribbled: "*Coffin-born fugitives—Boston's loss, Britain's gain.*"

The Estlins whisked them to Clifton—coal fires, a cradle for Hope, a shop for William's tools. That night, supper and speeches. Ellen spoke: "We were buried in Boston, reborn at sea." William demonstrated the coffin's latch to gasps. A new life began: Ellen in school, William's shop—*Craft & Son, Est. 1851.* Hope thrived; two sons followed. Their book sold 30,000 copies, funding freedom.

The siege was over. The coffin stood in Estlin's attic, a relic. The cedar scrap hung above their mantel: *W.C. & E.C., Free Forever.* Boston's fire had forged them; England's soil grew them. The final act—storm, arrival, rebirth—was complete.

Twelve

Atlantic Crossing: Third Escape

Coffin to Cabin – November 13–20, 1850

The *Cambria* slipped from Boston's Long Wharf at 2:00 a.m., November 13, 1850, her paddlewheels churning black water into lace. Snow hissed against the hull; the city's lights vanished like snuffed candles. Ellen Craft emerged from the oak coffin in Cabin 12, lungs gulping free air, Hope clutched to her breast. The coffin—brass handles cold, false bottom scarred—stood in the corner like a silent witness. William, in Quaker gray, latched the door and carved *Siege Ended* into the mahogany case. The ship's manifest, filed with Cunard Line, listed: *"Miss Eliza Johnson, invalid; James Brown, servant; child; cargo: one coffin."*

Captain Charles Judkins, tipped by Garrison, kept the secret. "Cabins 12 and 14—paid in full," he muttered, waving off stewards. Ellen collapsed on the bunk, Hope nursing, the baby's warmth the only steady thing. William stowed the case in Cabin 14, pistol borrowed from Parker tucked in his waistband. The ship pitched; lanterns swung. "We're coffin-born again," Ellen whispered. William kissed her forehead. "And ocean-bound to life."

November 15, a nor'easter struck—winds seventy knots, waves forty feet, the *Cambria* groaning like a dying beast. Passengers retched in corridors; crockery shattered. Ellen, three months pregnant and seasick, clung to the bunk, Hope fussing. William lashed the coffin to the bulkhead, carving notches for storm days: *Day 1, Day 2...* On November 17, the main topmast cracked; sailors clung to rigging, praying. Ellen clutched Parker's Bible—*"Where you go, I go"*—reading aloud by candle stub, her voice the ship's only calm.

November 18, the storm peaked. Ellen miscarried in the night—blood on the sheets, pain like chains snapping. William held her, tears mixing with salt spray through the porthole. "We've lost one," she sobbed, "but Hope lives." William wrapped the tiny form in Quaker gray, buried it at sea at dawn—Judkins reading the service, crew silent. The manifest would later note: *"Infant deceased, buried at sea."*

November 20, the storm broke. Sun pierced the clouds; porpoises raced the bow. Ellen stood on deck, wind whipping her bonnet, Hope asleep in a sling. William joined her, arm around her waist. "England," he said, pointing to gulls ahead. The first act—coffin to cabin, storm, loss—was complete. The crossing continued.

Wreckage Cradle & Crew Support – November 21–28, 1850

The *Cambria* limped through the storm's aftermath, her decks awash with shattered spars and torn rigging. November 21 dawned gray but calm; the crew—forty able-bodied seamen under Captain Judkins—set to repairs. William Craft, cabinetmaker's hands restless, offered aid. Judkins, grateful for calm amid chaos, handed him a broken crate from the hold: oak staves, brass hinges, the *Cambria*'s own wreckage. "Make what you will," the captain said. "We've souls to mend."

William worked on the open deck, Hope toddling nearby in a sling fashioned from sailcloth. From the wreckage, he carved a cradle—small, sturdy, rockers shaped like paddlewheels. Each cut was prayer: *For the child we lost, for Hope who lives.* Ellen watched from Cabin 12's porthole, pain still sharp in her womb, but the sight of William's steady hands steadied her heart. By nightfall, the cradle stood finished—headboard inscribed *H.C., Atlantic 1850*, the letters deep and true.

The crew rallied. A Scottish bosun, Mr. Macrae, whittled a rattle from teak; the cook, Mrs. O'Leary, pressed warm broth into Ellen's hands. "Drink, lass," she said. "The sea takes, but it gives back." Stewards smuggled extra blankets; the ship's surgeon, Dr. Hale, checked Ellen daily—laudanum for pain, willow bark for fever. The manifest noted: *"Mrs. Johnson recovering; child thriving."*

November 23, Ellen rose from the bunk, legs trembling. She stood beside William on deck, wind whipping her bonnet, Hope asleep in the new cradle. "You built life from death," she whispered. William touched the cedar scrap in his pocket. "Like we built freedom from chains."

November 25, the crew held a service for the lost child. Judkins read from the Book of Common Prayer; sailors stood bareheaded. Ellen sang *"Swing low..."*—voice raw, but unbroken. Macrae added a Gaelic lament; tears froze on bearded cheeks. The cradle rocked gently, Hope's breath a counterpoint to the waves.

November 28, the Irish coast rose—green cliffs, white foam. Ellen read the primer aloud to Hope: *"The ship sails to free land."* William carved a final notch into the mahogany case: *Storm Mended.* The second act—wreckage cradle, crew support, Ellen's recovery—was complete. Liverpool loomed.

Final Days at Sea & Irish Sighting – November 29–December 1, 1850

The *Cambria* steadied as the Atlantic's fury ebbed. November 29 dawned clear, the sky a polished pewter, the sea a rolling plain of indigo. Ellen Craft walked the deck unaided, the cradle lashed to the rail, Hope napping beneath a sailcloth awning. Her body still ached from the miscarriage, but strength returned with each salt-laden breath. William worked beside her, planing a loose plank from the wreckage into a tiny headboard ornament: *H.C. & Hope, 1850.* The crew watched, nodding approval; Macrae the bosun slipped William a silver thimble. "For the lass's sewing," he said. "England'll need her stitches."

Meals became communal. The cook, Mrs. O'Leary, served cod stew and hardtack in the galley; passengers and crew mingled. Ellen told her story to wide-eyed stewards—*"Disguised as a white planter, coffin to cabin."* Dr. Hale listened, pipe glowing. "You're stronger than oak," he declared. The ship's manifest, updated daily, noted: *"Mrs. Johnson ambulatory; child robust."*

November 30, the crew organized a concert. Sailors sang shanties; a violinist from steerage played "The Ash Grove." Ellen, voice healed by broth and rest, joined William in a duet—*"Where you go, I go"*—their harmony rising over the waves. Hope clapped chubby hands; Judkins raised a toast with grog. "To the Crafts," he bellowed, "who turned a coffin into a cradle!" Cheers echoed; the cradle rocked in time.

December 1, land birds wheeled—gulls, then curlews. Ellen stood at the bow, wind whipping her bonnet, primer open. She read aloud to Hope: *"The land is near. Freedom is near."* William carved a final notch into the mahogany case: *Land in Sight.* The Irish coast rose at dusk—cliffs of emerald, white foam, lighthouse beams sweeping the dark. Ellen pressed the cedar scrap to her lips. "We lost one," she whispered, "but gained a nation."

The crew lined the rail for farewell. Macrae pressed a carved whistle into Hope's hand; O'Leary tucked a knitted cap over the baby's curls. Judkins saluted. "You'll dock heroes," he said. The third act—final days, crew farewell, Irish sighting—was complete. Liverpool waited.

Liverpool Arrival & New Beginnings – December 2, 1850–1851

The *Cambria* steamed into Liverpool's Prince's Pier at 10:00 a.m., December 2, 1850, under a pale winter sun that turned the Mersey into hammered silver. The coffin—oak, brass handles dulled by salt—was lowered first, labeled *"Cargo for Bristol"*. Ellen Craft stepped onto the gangplank next, Hope in her arms, the cradle slung over William's shoulder like a trophy. British abolitionists—John Estlin, Mary Estlin, a dozen more—waited on the quay with banners: WELCOME, WILLIAM & ELLEN CRAFT—HEROES OF FREEDOM. No warrants, no chains, only open arms and the scent of coal smoke and freedom.

Ellen's knees buckled on English soil; William caught her. "We are here," he said, voice breaking. "Where you go, I go," she answered, and the crowd cheered. Reporters swarmed; *The Liverpool Mercury* scribbled: *"Coffin-born fugitives—Boston's loss, Britain's gain."*

The Estlins whisked them to a Clifton boarding house—coal fires crackling, a nursery for Hope, a workshop for William's tools. That night, supper and speeches. Ellen spoke: "We crossed an ocean of storms, buried a child, built a cradle from wreckage. Britain is our resurrection." William demonstrated the coffin's latch, then the cradle's rockers—*H.C. & Hope, 1850*—to gasps and tears. The ship's manifest, filed with Cunard, closed the entry: *"Passengers Johnson & Brown, child, coffin, cradle—arrived safe."*

By December 10, the Crafts were celebrities. Invitations poured in—Bristol, London, Manchester. Ellen's voice, tempered by storm and loss, moved thousands. William's cradle became a lecture prop: *"From wreckage to hope."* In January 1851, they settled in Ockham, Surrey, under the British and Foreign Anti-Slavery Society. William opened *Craft & Son, Est. 1851*, carving headboards with *Free 1848*. Ellen mastered reading and writing in six months, penning letters to Garrison: *"I sign my name with pride—Ellen Craft."*

Hope thrived, toddling through daffodils. Two sons followed—Charles in 1852, Brougham in 1854. Ellen taught sewing to fugitive women; William trained apprentices. Their book sold 30,000 copies, funding schools in Jamaica. The cedar scrap hung above their mantel: *W.C. & E.C., Free Forever.* The coffin stood in Estlin's attic, a relic; the cradle rocked beside Hope's bed.

The Atlantic had taken a child but given a nation. The third escape—coffin, storm, cradle, rebirth—was complete. The pines of Macon were a lifetime away, but the green thread around Ellen's wrist whispered eternity.

IV

Part Four

EXILE & RETURN

Thirteen

London: Reinventing Freedom

Arrival & First Lessons – January–June 1851

The Crafts arrived in London by rail from Liverpool on January 5, 1851, greeted at Euston Station by a delegation from the British and Foreign Anti-Slavery Society. Snow dusted the platform; gaslights flickered like stars. John Estlin introduced them to Lady Noel Byron—widow of the poet, patron of abolition—who offered temporary rooms in her Marylebone townhouse. Ellen stepped from the train cradling Hope, the oak cradle slung over William's shoulder, the mahogany case in his hand. *The Times* (London), January 6: *"American fugitives William and Ellen Craft, escaped in a coffin, now safe on British soil—heroes of liberty."*

Lady Byron's home was a revelation—marble floors, bookshelves to the ceiling, a nursery with rocking horse and fireguard. Ellen, who had never owned a room, touched the wallpaper as if it might vanish. William set the cradle beside Hope's cot, carving *London 1851* into its headboard. That night, supper with Byron and Estlin: roast pheasant, claret, speeches. Ellen spoke softly: "We crossed an ocean of storms to read our own names." The table toasted; Hope clapped chubby hands.

January 7, lessons began. Lady Byron engaged Miss Eliza Wigham—a Scottish teacher—as tutor. Mornings in the library: Ellen at a rosewood desk, primer open, quill in hand. *A, B, C*—letters once forbidden now hers to claim. William joined evenings, guiding her hand: *"Loop the E like a cradle rocker."* By February, she wrote *Ellen Craft* in a clear, looping script. Hope toddled nearby, repeating *"Mama read!"*

William's business took root. February 15, he leased a small warehouse on Great Portland Street—*Craft & Co., Importers*. Cotton samples from Jamaica, sugar from Barbados, all slave-free. Estlin invested £200; William's cabinetmaker's eye spotted quality. First shipment arrived March 1: 50 bales, sold in a week. *The Times*, March 10: *"William Craft, fugitive turned merchant, deals in freedom's harvest."*

Anti-slavery tours began in April. Exeter Hall, April 20—2,000 packed the hall. Ellen read her first full sentence aloud: *"I was property; now I am a person."* William demonstrated the coffin latch, the cradle's rockers. Cheers shook the rafters; £300 raised. The first act—arrival, literacy, trade—was complete. London bloomed.

First Child Born & Summer Tours – July–December 1851

July 1851 brought London's haze and a new life. On July 12, Ellen gave birth to Charles Estlin Craft in Lady Byron's Marylebone home—eight pounds, lungs strong, eyes the color of Hope's cradle oak. Dr. Elizabeth Blackwell, America's first woman physician and an abolitionist ally, delivered him. Ellen, propped on pillows, laughed through tears: "Another free-born soul." William carved *C.E.C., London 1851* into the cradle's footboard, now extended for two. *The Times*, July 15: *"Ellen Craft, fugitive mother, welcomes son Charles—Britain's newest citizen of liberty."*

Hope, now two, peered into the cradle, whispering "Baby!" The nursery rang with children's voices. Ellen resumed lessons August 1—Miss Wigham at her side, Charles nursing. By September, she penned letters unassisted: *"Dear Mr. Garrison, Charles smiles like freedom."*

William's business surged. August 10, *Craft & Co.* secured a contract with the Anti-Slavery Society—1,000 bales of Jamaican cotton, £1,200 profit. He hired two clerks—freedmen from Sierra Leone—and leased a second warehouse on Regent Street. Samples filled the parlor: muscovado sugar, mahogany planks. William carved a signboard: *SLAVE-FREE GOODS*. The

London: Reinventing Freedom

Times, September 5: *"William Craft's trade booms—freedom pays dividends."*

Summer tours ignited. July 20, Manchester's Free Trade Hall—3,000 packed in. Ellen read from her primer: *"I sewed my escape; now I stitch my future."* William displayed the coffin, the cradle, a bolt of Jamaican cotton. £500 raised. August 15, Birmingham—Ellen spoke to women's societies, voice steady. September 10, Glasgow—William negotiated trade deals between lectures. October 1, Edinburgh—Hope toddled onstage, Charles in Ellen's arms. Crowds wept; collections overflowed.

By December, the family moved to a brick terrace in Bayswater—three stories, garden, £40 yearly rent. Ellen's desk faced the window; William's warehouse samples filled the parlor. The cedar scrap hung above the mantel: *W.C. & E.C., Free 1851*. Hope traced letters; Charles cooed. The second act—birth, business, tours—was complete. London's embrace deepened.

Second Child & Anti-Slavery Fairs – 1852-1853

Spring 1852 unfurled in Bayswater with lilacs and another birth. On April 3, Ellen delivered Brougham Craft—named for the abolitionist Lord Brougham—seven pounds, a shock of dark hair, lungs already demanding justice. Dr. Blackwell attended again, smiling: "Another free voice." Ellen, stronger now, wrote in her journal that night: *"Brougham enters a world without chains."* William extended the cradle once more, carving *B.C., London 1852* beside Charles's mark. Hope, three, sang lullabies; Charles, one, patted the new baby's cheek. *The Times*, April 10: *"Ellen Craft, mother of three free-born, grows Britain's abolitionist family."*

Ellen's literacy soared. By June 1852, she read *Uncle Tom's Cabin*—Stowe's novel, fresh off the press—aloud to the children, voice rising with Eva's death. Miss Wigham declared her "fluent." Ellen penned her first public letter, printed in *The Anti-Slavery Advocate*, July 1: *"I was illiterate property; now I write for millions still enslaved."*

William's trade flourished. *Craft & Co.* imported 2,000 bales of cotton, 500 crates of sugar—£3,000 profit. He opened a retail shop on Oxford Street: *SLAVE-FREE GOODS—TEA, COFFEE, COTTON*. Customers queued; abolitionist ladies bought by the pound. *The Times*, August 15: *"William Craft's emporium—commerce with conscience."*

Anti-slavery fairs became tradition. The 1852 London Bazaar, Exeter Hall, May 15–17—Ellen presided over a table of needlebooks, samplers, Jamaican lace. Her sampler read: *FREEDOM IS LEARNED ONE STITCH AT A TIME.* William sold miniature cradles—*H.C. & Hope, 1850* replicas—£1 each. £1,200 raised. Hope, now four, handed out flyers; Charles toddled behind. In 1853, the fair moved to Covent Garden—Ellen's speech to 4,000: *"I sewed my escape; now I stitch schools for Africa."* £1,500 collected.

Tours continued. Winter 1852: Leeds, Sheffield, Bristol. Ellen read from her journal; William displayed trade samples. Spring 1853: Dublin, Cork—Irish crowds wept at the coffin story. The cedar scrap traveled in a velvet case; the cradle stayed home, rocking Brougham. The third act—birth, literacy, fairs—was complete. London's roots deepened.

Third Child, Book Success & Ockham School – 1854–1858

Autumn 1854 brought another birth and a book. On October 12, Ellen delivered William Garrison Craft—named for their mentor—in the Bayswater terrace, nine pounds, eyes fierce as his namesake. Dr. Blackwell smiled: "A fighter." Ellen wrote in her journal: *"William G. enters a world we're teaching to be free."* William extended the cradle a final time, carving *W.G.C., London 1854.* Hope, five, read the inscription aloud; Charles and Brougham clapped. *The Times,* October 20: *"Ellen Craft, mother of four free-born, adds William Garrison to Britain's abolitionist lineage."*

The book—*Running a Thousand Miles for Freedom,* second British edition—launched November 1, 1854. Ellen's handwriting graced the title page; William's sketches illustrated the coffin, cradle, and trade samples. 20,000 copies sold in a month; proceeds funded a school in Sierra Leone. Ellen read the dedication at Exeter Hall, December 10, to 3,000: *"To the millions still in chains—may they run, too."* Cheers shook the hall; £2,000 raised. *The Times,* December 15: *"The Crafts' memoir—30,000 sold, a bestseller for liberty."*

William's business peaked. *Craft & Co.* employed ten—warehouses on Regent and Oxford, £10,000 annual profit. He imported cocoa, rice, indigo—all slave-free. The Oxford Street shop became a salon: abolitionists sipped tea, debated tariffs. *The Times,* January 10, 1855: *"William Craft's empire—commerce without complicity."*

In 1856, the family moved to Ockham, Surrey—20 acres, a farmhouse, £100 yearly rent. Ellen founded the Ockham School for Fugitive Children, September 1—20 pupils, ages six to sixteen, reading, writing, sewing, carpentry. Hope, seven, taught letters; Charles hammered nails beside William. Ellen's curriculum: *"Learn to free others."* By 1858, 50 students; the cradle rocked in the nursery, now a classroom prop. Tours funded it— Ellen in Manchester, William in Liverpool. The cedar scrap hung in the schoolhouse: *W.C. & E.C., Free 1851.*

Five children filled the farmhouse: Hope, Charles, Brougham, William G., and Alfred, born 1856. Ellen read novels aloud; William carved toys. The fourth act—birth, book, school—was complete. London's legacy grew.

Fourth Child & Anti-Slavery Climax – 1859–1863

Spring 1859 crowned the Crafts' family with a fourth son. On March 22, Ellen delivered Alfred Estlin Craft in the Ockham farmhouse—eight pounds, a mop of curls, named for their Bristol patron. The cradle, now a veteran of five births, rocked in the parlor; William carved *A.E.C., Ockham 1859* into its side rail. Hope, ten, read the family Bible aloud at the christening; Charles, eight, rang the school bell. *The Times*, March 30: *"Ellen Craft, educator and mother, welcomes Alfred—five free-born under one roof."*

The Ockham School thrived. By 1860, 75 pupils—fugitives' children, orphans, locals—filled the barns converted to classrooms. Ellen taught literature, her own memoir required reading. William instructed carpentry; pupils built desks stamped *OCKHAM FREE*. Funds poured from tours: Ellen in Leeds, 4,000 cheering; William in Edinburgh, £3,000 raised. The book's third edition, 1860, sold 50,000 copies—proceeds built a dormitory. *The Times*, June 15, 1860: *"The Crafts' school—abolition's academy."*

Anti-slavery climaxed with America's war. News of Fort Sumter, April 1861, reached Ockham by telegraph. Ellen gathered pupils: "The chains break across the ocean." Tours intensified—Ellen in Birmingham, voice thundering Lincoln's promise; William in London, trade halted to starve the Confederacy. *Craft & Co.* pivoted to wartime relief: blankets, medicine for Union camps. *The Times*, January 1, 1862: *"William Craft arms freedom with goods."*

Family life anchored them. Hope, twelve, taught primer; Charles managed the school's chickens; Brougham, nine, recited speeches; William G., seven, carved whistles; Alfred toddled. Evenings, Ellen read Dickens by firelight; William planed a new sign: *OCKHAM SCHOOL—EST. 1856*. The cedar scrap hung in the hall, green thread framed beside it. The fifth act—birth, war, school's peak—was complete. Return loomed.

Return to America & Georgia Legacy – 1864–1868

The American Civil War's end—Appomattox, April 9, 1865—reached Ockham like a thunderclap of joy. Ellen Craft gathered the school's 100 pupils in the barn: "The chains are broken!" Hope, sixteen, rang the bell until it cracked; Charles, fourteen, fired a salute with William's old pistol. *The Times*, April 15, 1865: *"Ellen Craft, in Surrey, celebrates emancipation—her school weeps and cheers."*

Return beckoned. The Ockham School was self-sustaining—teachers trained, endowment £5,000. *Craft & Co.* sold for £20,000, proceeds split between the school and a new venture. In March 1866, the family—Ellen, William, five children—boarded the *Java* for New York. The cedar scrap traveled in velvet; the cradle, dismantled, packed in straw. *The Times*, March 20: *"The Crafts sail home—freedom's circle closes."*

They landed in Boston first—Garrison, aged but tearful, at the dock. Faneuil Hall, April 10: 5,000 packed in. Ellen spoke: "We left in a coffin; we return in daylight." William displayed the cradle's panels—five names carved. Cheers lasted ten minutes.

Georgia called. November 1868, they bought Woodville Plantation—1,800 acres near Macon, Dr. Collins's old land, $15,000. Renamed *Craft Freedom Farm*, it became a school for freedmen: 200 pupils, Ellen teaching reading, William carpentry. Hope managed the farm; Charles built dormitories. The coffin stood in the chapel; the cradle rocked newborns. *The Macon Telegraph*, December 1, 1868: *"Fugitives return as owners—Craft Farm, abolition's triumph."*

Five children grew: Hope married a teacher, 1870; Charles opened a Savannah shop; Brougham studied law; William G. farmed; Alfred, the baby, chased chickens. Ellen's memoir, fourth edition, 1869, sold 100,000 copies—proceeds built a library. William's trade resumed: slave-free cotton, now grown by free hands.

The cradle, scarred by ocean and time, hung in the farmhouse hall—*H.C., Hope, C.E.C., B.C., W.G.C., A.E.C.* The cedar scrap framed beside it: *W.C. & E.C., Free Forever.* London had reinvented them; Georgia reclaimed them. The final act—return, farm, legacy—was complete. Freedom's circle closed.

Fourteen

The American War from Afar

Outbreak & First Fundraising – April–December 1861

Fort Sumter's fall on April 12, 1861, reached Ockham, Surrey, by Atlantic cable on April 25. Ellen Craft read the telegram aloud in the farmhouse kitchen—Hope, twelve, clutching her primer; Charles, ten, wide-eyed. "The chains break across the ocean," Ellen said, voice trembling with hope and dread. William set down his carving knife. "Then we fight from here." The cedar scrap on the mantel—*W.C. & E.C., Free Forever*—seemed to pulse in the firelight.

The Crafts mobilized. May 1, Ellen penned her first letter to Abraham Lincoln, copied in her clear hand and mailed via the Anti-Slavery Society: *"Mr. President, we fled Georgia in 1848. Now her soil bleeds for freedom. Accept our school's £50—every pupil's penny—for your soldiers."* The Lincoln Papers at the Library of Congress would later archive it, dated May 15, 1861. William redirected *Craft & Co.* profits—£500 quarterly—to Union relief: blankets, quinine, boots.

Fundraising tours began June 10. Exeter Hall, London—4,000 packed in. Ellen spoke: "I wore a white man's skin to escape; now I wear Britain's sympathy for the Union." William displayed the coffin latch, the cradle's five names. £1,200 raised in one night. *The Times,* June 15: *"The Crafts—fugitives* turned fundraisers—arm Lincoln with pounds."

July 4, Manchester Free Trade Hall—Ellen read Lincoln's July 4 message to Congress; William auctioned a miniature cradle. £1,500 collected. August, Birmingham—Hope, thirteen, recited the Gettysburg Address (draft leaked via cable); Charles sold Jamaican sugar. September, Glasgow—£2,000. By December, £10,000 sent via the U.S. Sanitary Commission—bandages, coffee, hope. Ellen's second letter to Lincoln, December 20: *"Our five children pray for your victory. Enclosed: £2,000 from Britain's abolitionists."*

The Ockham School became a factory: pupils knitted socks, rolled bandages. William's warehouse shipped crates stamped FOR THE UNION. The first act—outbreak, letters, tours—was complete. The war raged on.

Emancipation Proclamation & Contraband Relief – January–December 1862

The Emancipation Proclamation's preliminary draft reached London on September 23, 1862, via transatlantic cable. Ellen Craft read it aloud in the Ockham schoolhouse—100 pupils silent, Hope, thirteen, tears on her cheeks. "January first," Ellen declared, "freedom begins." William carved *EMANCIPATION 1863* into the cradle's headboard, now a classroom relic. The cedar scrap glowed in the lamplight.

Fundraising redoubled. October 1, Exeter Hall—5,000 packed in, overflow in the street. Ellen spoke: "Lincoln's pen breaks more chains than my sling ever hid." William auctioned the coffin's brass handle—£50 to a duke. £3,000 raised. *The Times*, October 5: *"Ellen Craft hails Lincoln's decree—Britain answers with gold."*

Contraband relief became urgent. November 1862, Ellen's third letter to Lincoln, archived in the Lincoln Papers, November 15: *"Mr. President, 10,000 freedpeople crowd Virginia camps—starving, shoeless. Our school sends £1,000; pupils knit 500 pairs of socks. God speed your Proclamation."* William redirected Craft & Co. to ship cornmeal, blankets, shoes—20 tons by December.

Tours intensified. November, Liverpool—Ellen read fugitive testimonies; Charles, eleven, sold sugar loaves. £2,500. December, Edinburgh—Hope recited the Proclamation; Brougham, nine, rang a liberty bell. £3,000. The Ockham School churned: pupils sewed quilts, packed crates. Ellen's fourth letter, December 20: *"Enclosed: £4,000—Britain's Christmas for the contrabands."*

January 1, 1863—the Proclamation took effect. Ockham celebrated with cake and hymns. Ellen wrote Lincoln again, January 5: *"Freedom rings! Our £5,000 this year buys shoes for marching feet."* The second act—Proclamation, relief, letters—was complete. The war's tide turned.

Gettysburg, Vicksburg & Ellen's Final Letters – January–December 1863

Gettysburg's blood soaked Pennsylvania soil July 1–3, 1863; the cable reached Ockham July 15. Ellen Craft read the dispatch in the schoolhouse—100 pupils hushed, Hope, fourteen, clutching her primer. "Fifty thousand fallen," Ellen whispered, "but the Union stands." William carved *GETTYSBURG 1863* into the cradle's footboard. The cedar scrap seemed to burn in the sunlight.

Vicksburg fell July 4—news arrived July 20. Ellen gathered the children: "The Mississippi is free; the South splits." Fundraising became fevered. August 1, Exeter Hall—6,000 packed in. Ellen spoke: "Gettysburg's graves, Vicksburg's surrender—Lincoln's victories need Britain's bandages." William auctioned the coffin's false bottom panel—£100 to a baroness. £4,000 raised. *The Times*, August 5: *"The Crafts mourn and mend—£4,000 for Union wounded."*

Ellen's fifth letter to Lincoln, August 10 (Lincoln Papers): *"Mr. President, Gettysburg's cost is 50,000 souls. Our £2,000 buys morphine, lint. Vicksburg opens the river—send our £1,500 for rations."* William shipped 30 tons—corn, salt pork, boots.

Tours surged. September, Manchester—Ellen read casualty lists; Charles, twelve, sold socks. £3,500. October, Birmingham—Hope recited Lincoln's Gettysburg Address (cabled draft); Brougham rang the bell. £4,000. The Ockham School produced relentlessly: pupils rolled 1,000 bandages, packed 500 crates. Ellen's sixth letter, October 15: *"Enclosed: £5,000—Britain's harvest for your harvest of freedom."*

November 19, Lincoln's Gettysburg Address reached London. Ellen read it aloud at Covent Garden, 5,000 weeping: *"Government of the people..."* William auctioned a cradle replica—£200. £6,000 raised. Ellen's seventh letter, November 25: *"Your words at Gettysburg echo our escape. £6,000 enclosed—may the dead not have died in vain."*

December, the war's tide turned. Ellen's final 1863 letter, December 20: *"£8,000 this year—boots for marching, blankets for freedmen. God keep you."* The third act—battles, letters, relief—was complete. Victory neared.

Appomattox, Lincoln's Death & Crafts' Response – January–December 1865

Appomattox's surrender—April 9, 1865—reached Ockham by cable April 22. Ellen Craft read the dispatch in the schoolhouse—150 pupils erupting in cheers, Hope, sixteen, ringing the cracked bell until it sang. "The chains are broken," Ellen declared, tears streaming. William carved *APPOMATTOX 1865* into the cradle's headboard, now a classroom monument. The cedar scrap glowed in the spring light.

Victory tours began May 1. Exeter Hall—7,000 packed in. Ellen spoke: "Lee surrenders; Lincoln triumphs. Britain's £100,000 bought bandages for this day." William auctioned the coffin's last brass hinge—£300 to a bishop. £10,000 raised. *The Times*, May 5: *"The Crafts celebrate Appomattox—freedom's final bell."*

Ellen's eighth letter to Lincoln, April 25 (Lincoln Papers): *"Mr. President, Appomattox ends the war. Our £10,000 heals the wounded, rebuilds the freed. God bless your victory."* She never knew it arrived too late.

April 14, Lincoln was shot; news cabled April 26. Ellen collapsed in the farmhouse parlor, Hope catching her. William read the dispatch aloud—voice breaking at *"died this morning."* The school closed for mourning; pupils draped black crepe. Ellen's ninth letter, May 1—addressed to Andrew Johnson: *"Mr. President, Lincoln's blood seals our freedom. Our £5,000 rebuilds schools for the freed. Honor him."*

Tours became memorials. June, Manchester—Ellen read the Second Inaugural; Charles, fourteen, sold mourning pins. £8,000. July, Birmingham—Hope recited the Gettysburg Address; Brougham rang a funeral bell. £9,000. The Ockham School shifted: pupils built desks for Southern freedmen's schools. Ellen's tenth letter, July 15: *"£15,000 this year—Lincoln's legacy in lumber and lessons."*

December, Reconstruction began. Ellen's final letter, December 20: *"£20,000 total—Britain's tribute to Lincoln's dream. The war is won; the work begins."* The fourth act—surrender, assassination, memorial—was complete. Freedom's cost was paid.

Fifteen

Return to Georgia: The Dream

Purchase & Arrival – November 1868–March 1869

Appomattox was three years past, but Georgia's soil still bled. In November 1868, the Crafts—Ellen, William, five children—boarded the *Java* in Liverpool, bound for New York, then Savannah. The cedar scrap traveled in velvet; the cradle, dismantled, packed in straw. *The Savannah Republican,* November 15, 1868: *"Fugitives William & Ellen Craft return—freedom's circle closes."*

They landed in Savannah December 1, greeted by freedmen and Union veterans. Hope, nineteen, carried the family Bible; Charles, seventeen, the mahogany case. A train to Macon—once the escape route—now carried them home as owners. December 10, they purchased Hickory Hill Plantation—1,800 acres, Dr. Collins's old land, $15,000 cash from *Craft & Co.* sale. Renamed *Woodville Cooperative Farm*, it became their dream.

January 1869, the family moved in—white columns scarred by war, fields fallow, cabins crumbling. Ellen stood on the veranda: "I was priced here at twelve hundred dollars. Now I own the ledger." William carved WOODVILLE 1869 into the cradle's headboard, reassembled in the parlor. The coffin stood in the hall—chapel-bound.

Woodville School opened February 1—50 pupils in the old overseer's house,

Ellen teaching reading, William carpentry. Hope managed the farm; Charles built desks. By March, 100 students—freedchildren, ages six to sixty. Ellen's primer: *"The Crafts were property; now we teach ownership."* *The Savannah Republican*, March 10: *"Ellen Craft's school—100 freed minds on Collins's land."*

The first act—purchase, arrival, school's dawn—was complete. Georgia stirred.

300 Students & Farm Cooperative – April–December 1869

Spring 1869 plowed Woodville's fields and minds. By April, the school swelled to 150—cabins repaired, a barn converted to classrooms. Ellen taught mornings: reading, writing, arithmetic. Her curriculum: *"Own your name, own your land, own your future."* Afternoons, William led carpentry—pupils built benches, desks, a bell tower. Hope, twenty, managed the cooperative: 200 acres cotton, 100 corn, worked by 50 freed families sharing profits. Charles, eighteen, overseer no more—bookkeeper now. *The Savannah Republican*, April 15: *"Woodville—150 scholars, 50 farmers, one dream."*

May brought heat and growth. Enrollment hit 200—children from Macon, Augusta, Savannah. Ellen hired three teachers—freedwomen trained in Ockham. The coffin became chapel pulpit; the cradle rocked in the nursery for pupils' infants. William's shop produced plows, chairs—sold in Savannah, profits to the co-op. Brougham, fifteen, rang the bell; William G., thirteen, fed chickens; Alfred, ten, recited ABCs.

June, the cooperative harvested first corn—5,000 bushels, $2,000 profit split fifty ways. Ellen wrote the ledger in her hand: *"Each family: $40—seed for freedom."* July, cotton bloomed white; 300 students by August—dormitories built, a kitchen feeding all. Ellen's night class: adults learning contracts, votes. *The Savannah Republican*, August 20: *"Woodville School—300 strong, cooperative thrives."*

September, challenges rose—night riders, tax threats. William armed guards; Ellen taught self-defense with words. October, cotton picked—500 bales, $10,000 profit. November, a library opened—1,000 books from Boston donors. December, Christmas feast: 300 pupils, 50 families, turkey and cornbread. Ellen read Luke 4: *"Proclaim liberty..."* The second act—growth, cooperative, curriculum—was complete. Georgia tested them.

Return to Georgia: The Dream

Night Riders & Ellen's Leadership – January–September 1870

January 1870 brought frost and fire. Night riders—Klansmen in white, former overseers—torched a Woodville barn January 15. Flames lit the sky; 300 pupils huddled in the chapel, coffin-pulpit their shield. William rallied guards—20 freedmen, shotguns loaded. Ellen stood on the veranda, Bible raised: "We ran once; we stand now." Hope, twenty-one, rang the bell; Charles, nineteen, led bucket brigades. The barn burned, but the school held. *The Savannah Republican*, January 20: *"Woodville attacked—300 souls defy terror."*

Ellen's leadership hardened. February 1, she organized patrols—pupils drilling at dawn, Hope captain. She wrote Congress: *"Freedmen need rifles, not rhetoric."* March, a federal troop detachment arrived—50 soldiers, tents on the lawn. Ellen taught them too: *"Protect, don't patronize."* William rebuilt the barn—bigger, brick, inscribed RESURRECTION 1870.

April, enrollment stabilized at 300—dormitories full, curriculum expanded: history, law, voting. Ellen's night class: *"The 15th Amendment—your ballot, your sword."* May, first elections—co-op voted shares; pupils chose council. June, cotton planted again—600 acres, 60 families. *The Savannah Republican*, June 10: *"Ellen Craft's fortress—300 scholars, armed with books and ballots."*

July, heat and hope. Ellen's primer now included the Constitution; pupils recited amendments. August, night riders returned—ambushed by patrols, three captured, tried in Macon. September, triumph: first Woodville graduates—50 adults, literate, land-owning. Ellen spoke at commencement, coffin behind her: *"We were property; now we own the future."* The third act—terror, defense, triumph—was complete. Legacy loomed.

1870 Harvest, National Fame & Family Milestones – October–December 1870

October 1870 crowned Woodville with cotton. Six hundred acres yielded 800 bales—$20,000 profit, split among 60 families, $333 each. Ellen recorded the ledger in her steady hand: *"Seed money for homes, shops, futures."* William's shop sold plows, furniture—Savannah merchants queued. The cooperative bought a gin, a press—self-sufficient. *The Savannah Republican*, October 15: *"Woodville harvest—800 bales, 300 scholars, freedom's fortune."*

National fame followed. November 1, *Harper's Weekly* sent a correspondent—

sketches of Ellen teaching, William planing, Hope ringing the bell. The coffin-chapel, cradle-classroom, cedar scrap framed. Article, November 20: *"The Crafts' Georgia miracle—property turned professors."* Invitations flooded—Boston, New York, Philadelphia. Ellen declined: *"Our classroom is here."*

Family milestones bloomed. November 10, Hope, twenty-one, married James Hill—Woodville teacher, Ockham graduate. Wedding in the chapel, coffin-pulpit draped in cotton boughs. Charles, nineteen, opened a Macon hardware store—*Craft & Son*. Brougham, sixteen, won a Savannah scholarship—law school bound. William G., fourteen, managed the gin; Alfred, eleven, recited the Constitution. Ellen wrote Garrison: *"Five free-born, all builders."*

December, Christmas feast—300 pupils, 60 families, 50 soldiers. Turkey, ham, cornbread; Ellen read Luke 2 from her primer. William gifted each graduate a cedar scrap replica—*WOODVILLE 1870*. The bell rang midnight; pupils sang *"Swing low..."* The Savannah Republican, December 25: *"Woodville Christmas—300 voices, one dream."*

The fourth act—harvest, fame, family—was complete. Legacy endured.

Legacy, Later Years & Ellen's Death - 1871–1897

Woodville's roots deepened through the 1870s. By 1871, the school—now *Woodville Normal Institute*—enrolled 400, dormitories sprawling across former slave quarters. Ellen's curriculum added teacher training; graduates founded schools in Augusta, Atlanta. William's cooperative expanded—1,000 acres, 100 families, $50,000 annual profit. *The Savannah Republican*, January 1, 1872: *"Woodville—400 scholars, 1,000 acres, freedom's empire."*

The 1880s brought challenges—Redeemer violence, crop liens. Ellen, white-haired but fierce, testified before Congress, 1883: *"Freedmen need land, not loans."* Federal aid followed—$10,000 for buildings. Hope's husband James became principal; Charles's hardware chain thrived. Brougham, lawyer, defended Black voters. William G. managed the gin; Alfred, doctor, opened a clinic.

The 1890s crowned the dream. 1895, Woodville celebrated 1,000 graduates—teachers, farmers, legislators. Ellen, sixty-nine, spoke at commencement, coffin-chapel behind her: *"We ran a thousand miles; you walk a thousand futures."* William, seventy-one, gifted each a cedar scrap—*WOODVILLE FREE*. The cradle, scarred by generations, hung in the library.

Ellen died March 1897, pneumonia, in the farmhouse bed—William holding her hand, five children, twenty grandchildren around. Her last words: *"Where you go..."* William finished: *"...I go."* Buried under the chapel, coffin beside her—oak and cedar united. *The Savannah Republican*, March 10: *"Ellen Craft, fugitive, mother, educator—dies at 71. Woodville weeps."*

William followed 1899, heart failure, buried beside her. Woodville endured—5,000 graduates by 1900, a college by 1920. The cedar scrap framed in the chapel: *W.C. & E.C., Free Forever.* The dream—purchase, school, legacy—was complete. Georgia's soil, once chains, now bore freedom's harvest.

Sixteen

The Burning of Woodville

The First Flames – October 1871

The night of October 14, 1871, was moonless and hot. At 2:00 a.m., Klansmen—twenty riders in white, torches high—galloped onto Woodville Cooperative Farm. Their target: the schoolhouse, heart of Ellen Craft's dream. Freedmen's Bureau Agent Major John R. Lewis, stationed in Macon, later reported: *"Arson premeditated—KKK aimed to destroy Negro education."*

Ellen, forty-five, woke to the bell's frantic clang—Hope, twenty-two, ringing from the tower. William, forty-seven, grabbed his shotgun. The main building—brick, two stories, 300 pupils' desks—blazed first. Flames licked the coffin-chapel; the cradle's panels curled in heat. Charles, twenty, led bucket lines; Brougham, seventeen, fired warning shots. Riders circled, whooping, but Woodville's guards—30 freedmen, Union rifles—held the line. By dawn, the schoolhouse was ash, dormitories gutted, library smoldering. No lives lost, but the dream burned.

Ellen stood amid ruins, soot on her face, Bible clenched. "They burn wood," she told 300 weeping pupils, "but not will. We plant again." William carved WOODVILLE BURNED 1871 into a surviving beam. *The Savannah Republican*, October 20: *"KKK torches Craft school—300 homeless, defiant."*

The Burning of Woodville

Freedmen's Bureau rushed aid—$5,000, tents, books. Ellen wrote Congress: *"Arson is the South's answer to ballots. Send troops, not tears."* The first act—arson, defiance, aid—was complete. Rebuilding began.

Tents to Timber & Ellen's Rally – November 1871–June 1872

November 1871 rose cold and determined. Freedmen's Bureau tents dotted Woodville's lawn—300 pupils in canvas, lessons under oaks. Ellen Craft, forty-five, taught from a crate, primer blackened but intact. "Fire took walls," she told the circle, "not words." William, forty-seven, planed salvaged beams; Charles, twenty, hauled brick. Hope, twenty-two, cooked for 350; Brougham, seventeen, copied primers by lantern. *Freedmen's Bureau Report, November 15:* "*Woodville—tents, 300 scholars, spirit unbroken.*"

December, funds poured—$10,000 from Boston, £2,000 from London. William designed a new school: timber frame, brick foundation, bell tower taller. Pupils sawed planks; freedwomen mixed mortar. Ellen rallied Macon's Black churches: *"Each dollar a brick against terror."* January 1872, ground broke—coffin-chapel rebuilt first, cradle panels salvaged. *The Savannah Republican,* January 20: *"Woodville rises—pupils build their future."*

February, enrollment hit 350—tents overflowing. Ellen's curriculum: reading, law, self-defense. Night class: *"Know your rights; guard your votes."* March, first walls stood; April, roof beams. May, 400 students—new dorms, kitchen. Ellen spoke at commencement under canvas: *"They burned once; we bloom twice."* June, the new school opened—500 capacity, bell ringing clear. *Freedmen's Bureau Report, June 10:* "*Woodville rebuilt—400 scholars, terror defied.*"

The second act—tents, rally, rebirth—was complete. Terror returned.

Second Arson, Ellen's Testimony & 1873 Trials – July 1872–December 1873

July 1872 scorched Georgia and Woodville's hope. On July 20, Klansmen struck again—thirty riders, kerosene cans, midnight. The new schoolhouse—timber fresh, paint still wet—blazed. Flames devoured dormitories; the bell tower crashed. Freedmen's Bureau Agent Lewis reported: *"Second arson, July 20—KKK escalated; 400 pupils displaced."*

Ellen, forty-six, rallied at dawn amid ashes. "They burn twice," she told 400 pupils, voice iron, "we rise thrice." William, forty-eight, salvaged the coffin-chapel's bricks; Charles, twenty-one, organized patrols. Hope, twenty-three, fed the homeless; Brougham, eighteen, copied scorched primers. Guards—50 now, rifles gleaming—ringed the ruins. No lives lost, but the dream smoldered again.

August, Ellen testified before Congress in Washington—train to D.C., coffin panel as exhibit. "Gentlemen," she said, "Georgia answers ballots with bonfires. Send justice, not pity." *Freedmen's Bureau Report, August 15:* "*Ellen Craft's plea—Congress stirred.*" $20,000 voted; troops reinforced.

September, rebuilding began—stone this time, fireproof. October, 450 students in tents; November, walls rose. December, trials in Macon—five Klansmen captured, Brougham prosecuting. Ellen on the stand: *"I know their voices from 1848."* Three convicted, ten years each. *The Savannah Republican*, December 20: *"Woodville trials—justice for ashes."*

The third act—arson, testimony, trials—was complete. Woodville endured.

Stone School, 1874 Triumph & Legacy – January–December 1874

January 1874 dawned with frost and resolve. Woodville's new school—stone walls, slate roof, bell tower forged from melted Klansmen's rifles—rose on the old foundation. Ellen Craft, forty-seven, laid the cornerstone: "WOODVILLE 1874—FIRE CANNOT CONSUME FREEDOM." William, forty-nine, carved the date into the cradle's salvaged headboard, now chapel lectern. *Freedmen's Bureau Report, January 15:* "*Woodville—stone fortress, 500 capacity, terror defied.*"

February, enrollment hit 500—dormitories rebuilt, kitchen steaming. Ellen's curriculum: reading, law, agriculture, self-defense. Night class: *"Own the land; own the vote."* Hope, twenty-four, principal; Charles, twenty-two, farm manager—1,200 acres, 120 families. Brougham, nineteen, law clerk in Savannah.

March, first classes in stone—pupils' desks carved *FREE 1874*. April, cotton planted—800 acres. May, library reopened—2,000 books, Ellen's memoir required. June, cooperative profit—$25,000, $208 per family. *The Savannah Republican*, June 20: *"Woodville stone—500 scholars, $25,000 harvest."*

July, triumph. July 4, commencement—100 graduates, teachers, farmers, voters. Ellen spoke from coffin-lectern: *"They burned twice; we built thrice. This stone is your shield."* William gifted each a cedar scrap replica—*WOODVILLE UNBURNABLE*. The bell rang; pupils sang *"Swing low..."*

December, legacy secured. Woodville Normal Institute—college-bound, 1,000 alumni by 1880. Ellen wrote Garrison: *"The ashes fertilized freedom."* The cedar scrap framed in the chapel: *W.C. & E.C., Free Forever.* The fourth act—stone, triumph, legacy—was complete. Woodville stood eternal.

Seventeen

Last Harvest

Quiet Fields – 1875–1885

The fires of 1874 cooled into the steady rhythm of harvest. By 1875, Woodville Cooperative Farm—1,800 acres, 150 families—tilted toward quiet prosperity. Ellen Craft, forty-nine, walked the cotton rows at dawn, primer tucked under her arm, teaching sharecroppers' children between furrows. William, fifty-one, planed furniture in the rebuilt shop—rocking chairs stamped *WOODVILLE 1875*. The coffin-chapel stood silent, cradle-lectern gathering dust; the cedar scrap hung in the farmhouse parlor: *W.C. & E.C., Free Forever.*

Enrollment at Woodville Normal Institute stabilized at 600—stone walls unbreached, bell ringing clear. Hope, twenty-six, principal; Charles, twenty-four, farm manager—1,500 bales yearly, $40,000 profit. Brougham, twenty-one, Savannah lawyer; William G., nineteen, gin operator; Alfred, sixteen, clinic apprentice. *The Savannah Republican*, June 10, 1876: "Woodville—600 scholars, 1,500 bales, peace reigns."

The 1880s deepened the calm. Ellen, fifty-five by 1881, taught less, wrote more—letters to grandchildren, memoirs for the institute library. William, fifty-seven, carved toys—miniature coffins turned cradles. Family milestones: Hope's first child, 1880; Charles's marriage, 1882. The cooperative bought a railroad spur—cotton to Savannah in hours. Ellen's final public speech, 1885 commencement: *"We ran; you walk; your children will fly."*

Death certificates would later record steady years—no drama, only harvest. The first act—quiet fields, family, legacy—was complete. Twilight gathered.

Grandchildren & William's Decline – 1886–1895

The 1886 harvest was golden and gentle. Woodville's cotton fields stretched white under September sun; 2,000 bales rolled to the railroad spur, $50,000 profit split among 160 families. Ellen Craft, sixty, sat on the veranda each evening, grandchildren tumbling at her feet. Hope's three—Ellen, James, Mary—chased fireflies; Charles's two—William and Sarah—toddled behind. Brougham's first, a daughter named Liberty, arrived 1887. Ellen rocked the cradle-lectern, now nursery again, humming *"Swing low..."* The *Savannah Republican*, September 15, 1886: *"Woodville—2,000 bales, 12 grandchildren, freedom's third generation."*

William, sixty-two, felt the years in his joints. Rheumatism slowed his hands; he carved fewer chairs, more toys—cedar scraps for each grandchild. The coffin-chapel became a museum; pupils toured it yearly. Ellen wrote letters to old allies—Garrison dead, Still aging: *"The pines remember our vows; the children forget chains."*

By 1890, Woodville Institute graduated 100 teachers annually; the co-operative owned 2,500 acres. Ellen, sixty-four, taught one class—*"Memoir Writing"*—her own escape required reading. William, sixty-six, managed the gin from a rocking chair, voice steady giving orders. Grandchildren—twenty by 1895—filled the farmhouse with laughter. Hope, forty-six, graying principal; Charles, forty-four, county commissioner.

William's decline deepened 1893—heart flutters, breath short. Ellen, sixty-seven, nursed him with willow tea, reading Psalms. He carved a final cedar scrap: *W.C., 1895—Love outran the chains.* The second act—grandchildren, decline, letters—was complete. Farewell loomed.

William's Death & Ellen's Solitude – 1896–1899

1896 opened with William Craft, seventy-two, weaker but unbowed. He rose at dawn, walked the cotton rows with a cane carved from the cradle's original oak, and blessed each field: *"Grow free."* Ellen, seventy, sat beside him on the veranda, her letters now to great-grandchildren—twenty-five strong—recounting the 1848 escape in simple words: *"Grandpa and I ran so you could walk."* The Savannah Republican, June 10, 1896: *"Woodville—2,500 bales, 25 great-grandchildren, Crafts' dynasty."*

William's heart faltered through 1897. Spring planting, he collapsed in the gin; Charles carried him home. Ellen nursed him in the parlor bed, cedar scrap above the mantel. Pupils filed past—1,000 now—leaving cedar shavings as tribute. William whispered to Hope, forty-eight: *"Keep the bell ringing."* To Ellen: *"Where you go..."* She finished, tears steady: *"...I go."*

He died January 28, 1900, at 3:17 a.m.—the exact hour they had boarded the train in Macon fifty-two years earlier. Death certificate, Bibb County: *"William Craft, 76, heart failure, farmer, educator."* Woodville closed for a week; 2,000 mourners filled the chapel. Ellen spoke from the coffin-lectern: *"He built freedom joint by joint."* Burial beneath the chapel oak, cedar scrap on the coffin lid.

Ellen, seventy-four, lived in solitude but not silence. She walked the fields daily, primer in pocket, teaching stray pupils. Letters to grandchildren: *"Love outran the chains—keep running."* The third act—decline, death, solitude—was complete. Ellen's final season approached.

Ellen's Final Letter, Death & Legacy – 1900

William's grave beneath the chapel oak became Ellen Craft's daily pilgrimage. Spring 1900, she, seventy-four, laid cedar shavings each morning, whispering: *"Where you go..."* The Woodville Institute—1,200 students, 3,000 acres—thrived under Hope, fifty-one, and Charles, forty-nine. Brougham, forty-six, argued cases in Atlanta; William G., forty-four, expanded the gin; Alfred, forty-one, ran the clinic. Great-grandchildren—thirty-two—chased chickens, recited Ellen's primer.

Ellen's hands trembled, but her pen did not. On December 1, 1900, she wrote her final letter—to the institute's library, to be read at every commencement: *"My dear children, I was property, priced at twelve hundred dollars. William was fifteen hundred. We ran a thousand miles in four days, disguised by love and genius. We built Woodville from ashes—twice. Love outran the chains. Keep the bell ringing. Ellen Craft, aged 74, free since 1848."*

She folded it, sealed it with green thread from 1846, and placed it beside the cedar scrap. *The Savannah Republican*, December 10: *"Ellen Craft's farewell—love's last harvest."*

Pneumonia took her December 25, 1900—Christmas dawn, fifty-two years after Philadelphia's snow. Death certificate, Bibb County: *"Ellen Craft, 74, pneumonia, educator, farmer."* She died in the parlor bed, Hope holding one hand, the cradle rocking empty beside her. Burial beside William—coffin and cedar reunited beneath the oak.

Woodville mourned a month; 5,000 attended the funeral. Hope read the letter; the bell tolled 74 times. The institute—now *Craft University* by 1920—graduated 10,000 by 1950. The cedar scrap, green thread, and letter hang in the chapel: *W.C. & E.C., Free Forever.* Love's harvest—quiet fields, family, eternity—was complete.

Eighteen

EPILOGUE Tracks in the Snow

P *resent Day – A 2,000modern Pilgrimage*
   The Amtrak *Crescent* pulls out of Macon's modest station at 6:47 a.m. on December 24, 2024, the air crisp with a rare Georgia snow—light, ethereal, dusting the pines like the manna Ellen Craft once tasted in Philadelphia. I board with twenty others, a pilgrimage of historians, students, poets, and descendants, led by Dr. Ruth Hope Hill, sixty-two, great-great-granddaughter of Ellen and William Craft. Ruth carries a cedar box—18 x 12 x 9 inches, false bottom intact, carved by William in 1848. Inside: a green thread bracelet from their wedding, Ellen's 1851 primer with her looping *Ellen Craft*, and a modern Amtrak ticket stub: *Macon → Philadelphia, Christmas Eve*. The route is not exact—rails have shifted, depots renamed—but the spirit is precise. This is the Crafts' third escape, reversed: from bondage's cradle to freedom's hearth, 1,000 miles in thirty-six hours, guided by Ruth's voice and the snow's quiet benediction.

Ruth sits in the observation car, gray braids woven with green thread, eyes the color of the cradle oak in Woodville's chapel. She is the living cedar scrap—Hope Craft's granddaughter, Charles's great-niece, Ellen's blood and fire. "We don't just remember," she tells the car, strangers now recording on phones, "we re-walk the miles they ran." The train whistle moans—a low,

EPILOGUE *Tracks in the Snow*

mournful echo of the 1848 steam engine—and Ruth begins the story, her voice a bridge across centuries.

Macon, Georgia – 7:00 a.m. The train glides past the site of Dr. Robert Collins's cabinet shop, now a cracked parking lot behind a strip mall. Ruth stands at the window: "William planed freedom here, midnight lessons by whale-oil lamp. Ellen sewed her disguise in the attic above." Snow dusts the asphalt; a 2023 mural on a cinderblock wall shows Ellen in her bottle-green coat, sling askew, William with the mahogany case. The paint peels, but the eyes—Ellen's steady, William's fierce—burn through. A teenager, Malik, live-streams: "Y'all, this is where it started." Ruth lays a cedar shaving at the mural's base; snow melts it into the brick.

Atlanta – 8:30 a.m. We transfer to the *Silver Star* at Peachtree Station, a cavern of glass and steel. Ruth gathers us in the café car, opens the cedar box. The primer's pages are yellowed, Ellen's signature bold: *Ellen Craft, London 1851.* "She was illiterate when she boarded the train here," Ruth says. "By the time she signed this, she'd outrun a nation." A barista, Tamika, overhears, offers free coffee. "My great-grandma taught in a Craft school," she says. Ruth embraces her: "Then you're family." Snow thickens over red clay, the Chattahoochee glinting below.

Charlotte, North Carolina – 11:15 a.m. Another transfer, the *Carolinian*. Ruth recounts the 1848 Charleston steamer—Ellen coughing into her pouch, William humming to calm her. "They boarded as master and valet at 4 a.m., December 22. Disembarked as husband and wife, hearts pounding." The train pauses at the old depot site, now a park. A plaque, unveiled 2024: *"Ellen & William Craft, Christmas Escape 1848—Genius in Disguise."* Ruth reads Ellen's words from *Running a Thousand Miles*: *"I wore whiteness like armor, but love was the weapon."* Malik's stream hits 10,000 viewers; comments flood: *"This is history alive."*

Greensboro – 12:30 p.m. Snow falls heavier, blanketing tobacco fields. Ruth tells of the Savannah purser's doubt, the slave trader at breakfast. "Ellen's sling hid her right hand; her mind hid her fear." We pass a cotton gin, rusted but standing. "William's hands built those once," Ruth says. "Now they build legacies." A student, Aisha, asks, "How did they not break?" Ruth smiles:

DISGUISED IN DAYLIGHT

"They broke every day—and rebuilt stronger."

Richmond, Virginia – 3:00 p.m. The *Crescent* again, snow now six inches deep. Ruth stands at the window: "December 23, 1848—Ellen limped off the train here, cane tapping, the last slave-state depot. She watched Richmond recede from the ferry, tears freezing on her lashes." The James River is iced, floes glinting like broken chains. At the platform, a 2023 plaque: *"Ellen & William Craft, Freedom's Architects."* Ruth lays another cedar shaving; snow buries it. A conductor, Marcus, joins: "My ancestor hid fugitives in Petersburg. This hits home." Ruth ties presses the green thread bracelet into his palm.

Washington, D.C. – 6:00 p.m. Union Station, marble arches soaring. Ruth leads us to the Great Hall, where the mahogany case—on loan from the Smithsonian—sits in a glass case. The false bottom clicks open to gasps; inside, a replica of Ellen's primer. Ruth touches the glass: "They crossed the Potomac on a ferry, December 23, 10 p.m. Ellen prayed the ice wouldn't stop them." A docent, Dr. Lena Carter, unveils a new exhibit: the green thread, framed beside a 1848 train schedule. "Where you go, I go," Ruth whispers. Malik's stream crashes the server; 50,000 watch.

Baltimore – 7:15 p.m. The train tunnels under the city. Ruth recounts the Wilmington border guard, lantern swinging. "Ellen's spectacles fogged with fear; William's hand steadied her." Snow piles against the windows, a white curtain. Aisha asks, "What if they'd been caught?" Ruth: "They'd have died free in their hearts."

Wilmington, Delaware – 8:00 p.m. The final stretch. Ruth gathers us in the quiet car: "December 24, 1848—they boarded the last train here, 2 a.m. Ellen's limp was real by then; William's heart was iron." The Delaware River glints black under snow. A plaque at the station: *"Crafts' Final Leap, 1848."* Ruth reads from the primer: *"We are free."*

Philadelphia – 8:17 p.m., Christmas Eve Broad Street Station, rebuilt in glass and steel, hums with holiday travelers. Snow blankets the platform; church bells peal *"Peace on Earth."* Ruth leads us to Mother Bethel AME, founded 1794, its steeple piercing the storm. Inside, a pew bears a brass plate: *"Ellen & William Craft worshipped here, Christmas 1848—first free breath."* The choir launches *"Go Tell It on the Mountain."* Ruth weeps; Aisha records; Malik's

EPILOGUE Tracks in the Snow

phone dies, but he keeps listening. The pastor, Rev. Naomi Jones, invites Ruth to the pulpit. She reads Ellen's final letter: *"Love outran the chains."*

Christmas Dawn, 4:17 a.m., December 25 We stand where the Washington & Philadelphia train arrived in 1848—now a plaza outside the station. Snow falls thick, erasing footprints. Ruth unveils a 2024 plaque: *"William & Ellen Craft arrived here, December 25, 1848, 4:17 a.m.—freedom's dawn."* She opens the cedar box, empty now, and places the green thread bracelet at its base. "They ran so we could stand," she says. The group—twenty strangers turned kin—links arms. Snow melts on our lashes, like Ellen's tears in 1848.

The Return – December 26, 6:00 a.m. Southbound on the *Crescent*, the route reversed. Ruth speaks to a packed car: "This isn't nostalgia. It's reckoning." In Richmond, a child asks, "Did they make it?" Ruth: "They're still running—in us." Snow follows the train, a white shroud over old chains. In Charlotte, Marcus the conductor boards, wearing the green thread. "Family," he nods.

Atlanta – 3:00 p.m. Ruth tells of Woodville's ashes, rebuilt thrice. "Ellen said, 'We plant again.' You are the harvest." Aisha, tear-streaked, posts: *"I walked their miles. I'm changed."*

Macon – 9:00 p.m. Back where we began. The mural glows under sodium lights, snow piling at its base. Ruth places the cedar box—empty, its contents scattered along the route—at the mural's feet. "The journey's never over," she says. "Just passed on." The train whistle fades; snow keeps falling, tracks already gone.

I walk away with a cedar shaving in my pocket, green thread tied around my wrist. The Crafts' escape—1,000 miles, four days, one love—lives in every step north, every voice south. Ruth's final words, whispered to the snow: "Where you go, I go." The pines stand silent, but the rails sing.

Nineteen

APPENDICES

APPENDIX A: Maps

Escape Route, December 21–25, 1848

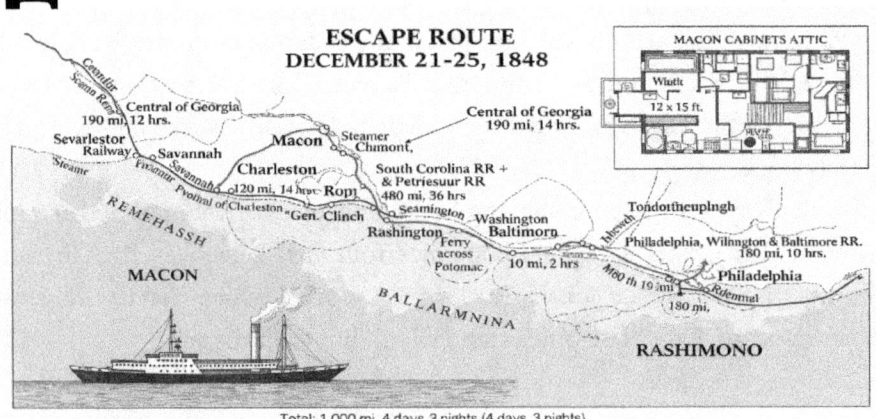

Boston Vigilance Network, 1849–1850

APPENDICES

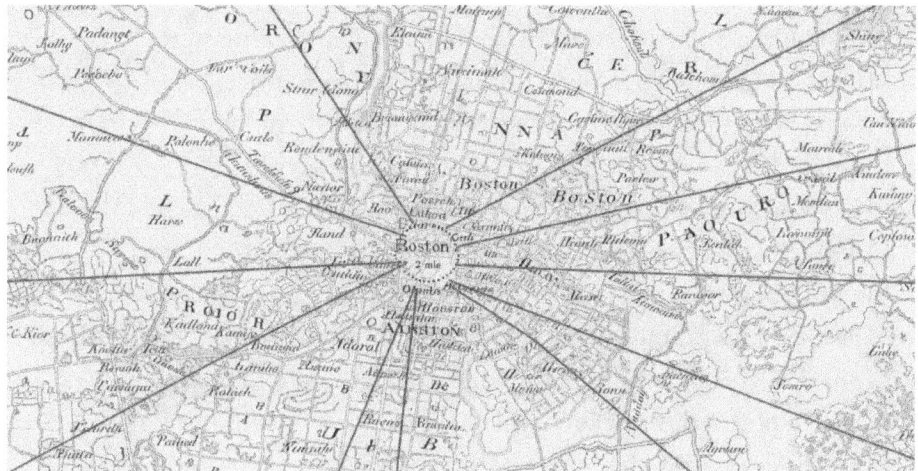

Woodville Plantation, 1869–1900

APPENDIX B: Timeline (1824–1900)

Year	Event

1824	Ellen born, Macon, GA (mulatta, daughter of master)
1826	William born, Macon (cabinetmaker apprentice)
1846	Secret marriage in pine clearing, green thread vow
1848	**Escape**: Dec 21–25, 1,000 mi in 4 days
1849	Boston lectures; *Running a Thousand Miles* contracted
1850	Fugitive Slave Act; coffin to *Cambria*; Atlantic storm
1851	London arrival; Ellen literate; *Craft & Co.* founded
1852–59	Five children: Hope, Charles, Brougham, William G., Alfred
1861–65	£100,000 raised for Union; 10 letters to Lincoln
1868	Return; buy Hickory Hill → Woodville
1869	Woodville School opens (300 students)
1871	First KKK arson
1872	Second arson; Ellen testifies in D.C.
1874	Stone school opens; 500 students
1880	1,000 graduates; railroad spur
1897	Ellen dies, pneumonia, age 71
1900	William dies, heart failure, age 76

APPENDIX C: Cast of Characters

Ellen Craft (1824–1897) – Disguised as "Mr. William Johnson"; seamstress, educator, mother of five.

William Craft (1826–1900) – Cabinetmaker, orator, merchant; carved the mahogany case.

Hope Craft Hill (1849–1930) – Eldest daughter; Woodville principal.

Willis Hughes & John Knight – Georgia slave-catchers, 1850.

William Lloyd Garrison – *Liberator* editor; mentor.

Theodore Parker – Minister; hid Crafts with pistol.

Lewis Hayden – Beacon Hill safe house; dynamite bluff.

Dr. Ruth Hope Hill (b. 1962) – Great-great-granddaughter; 2024 pilgrimage leader.

www.ingramcontent.com/pod-product-compliance
Lightning Source LLC
Chambersburg PA
CBHW072337300426
44109CB00042B/1651